THE EPIC BOOK OF KID LIFE SKILLS AWESOMENESS

HOW TO COOK, CLEAN, MANAGE MONEY,
LEARN INTERNET AND BODY SAFETY, AND
HANDLE BIG FEELINGS FOR TWEENS AGES 8-12

Audrey Coffie

© Copyright Audrey Coffie 2023 - All rights reserved.

The content contained within this book may not be reproduced, duplicated, or transmitted without direct written permission from the author or the publisher.

Under no circumstances will any blame or legal responsibility be held against the publisher, or author, for any damages, reparation, or monetary loss due to the information contained within this book. Either directly or indirectly. You are responsible for your own choices, actions, and results.

Legal Notice:

This book is copyright protected. This book is only for personal use. You cannot amend, distribute, sell, use, quote, or paraphrase any part of the content within this book without the consent of the author or publisher.

Disclaimer Notice:

Please note that the information contained within this document is for educational and entertainment purposes only. All effort has been executed to present accurate, up-to-date, reliable, and complete information. No warranties of any kind are declared or implied. Readers acknowledge that the author is not engaging in the rendering of legal, financial, medical, or professional advice. The content within this book has been derived from various sources. Please consult a licensed professional before attempting any techniques outlined in this book.

By reading this document, the reader agrees that under no circumstances is the author responsible for any losses, direct or indirect, which are incurred as a result of the use of the information contained within this document, including, but not limited to, — errors, omissions, or inaccuracies.

CONTENTS

INTRODUCTION	V
FOOD FIRST: EASY COOKING HACKS YOU SHOULD KNOW	1
SPICK AND SPAN: DOING CHORES WHILE STILL HAVING FUN	17
MONEY MATTERS: HOW TO SECURE THE BAG	35
MORE THAN STRANGER DANGER: LEARNING THE ROPES OF PERSONAL SAFETY	49
EMO DUMPS: MANAGING EMOTIONS EFFECTIVELY	63
GLOW UP: STRIVING FOR SELF-IMPROVEMENT	77
IN CASE OF EMERGENCY: HOW TO BE A REAL LIFE SUPERHERO	89
CONCLUSION	101

INTRODUCTION

Say goodbye to babysitters, kiddy cups at restaurants, and being banned from the "adult" table, and hello to middle school, new interests, and a big ole' scoop of independence.

If you're reading this, you've likely entered the world of being a tween. For that, I'm thrilled to say congratulations and welcome to the start of some of the most exciting times of your life! Let me prepare you; things are going to happen QUICKLY. You know how people say that "life goes by fast?" Consider your tween years chapter one of life hopping on the fast track, so remember to appreciate each day and, most importantly, have fun.

As you read this book, you can start to get a feel of what to expect during this time in your life, as well as ways to make the most of the best parts and get through the hard parts. I get it; this may sound a tad bit intimidating, I've been here too, and I want you to know that all your feelings are valid, completely normal, and welcome here.

Think of your tween life as a character in your favorite tv show. For example, *Highschool Musical: The Musical Series*, *Rise of the Teenage Mutant Ninja Turtles*, *Stranger Things*, etc.

If you compare the first episode to the last, how have they changed? Do they have the same interests, friends, or goals? If I had to guess, you're probably shaking your head no right now. Like the show, each person goes through different things in life that cause social, emotional, and physical changes. During your tween years, these changes will very likely happen more than just once or twice – but that's exactly why it's exciting!

Since the time you were born, your family members are the people you've been around the most, which means a lot of the things you do, the clothes you wear, and the ways you act have been influenced by your family. Since you're a tween now, you'll have more independence to decide who you spend time with than when you were a kid. These new people may have different hobbies, likes, and dislikes, and suddenly you'll find yourself loving a new sport that you've never even heard of before. During the next few years as a tween, you'll constantly be around new types of people, try new things, and discover what you truly enjoy.

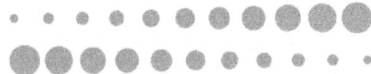

Sounds pretty cool, right? Well, it gets even better. Being a kid means that everything around you is done for you by adults, which can be nice sometimes, but it also means that you don't have a say in really anything. The food you eat, the clothes you wear, and exactly when you go to bed at night and wake up in the morning is all decided by your parents. However, as a tween, the time has come that people will begin to trust you with responsibilities. Yes, this does include cleaning your room, washing your dinner plate, and feeding the dog, but it also means that whether you wear socks with your sneakers, the time you do (or don't do) your homework, and if you have chips or a sandwich for breakfast is decided by you.

It's important to remember that choosing not to do the right thing with this new responsibility and independence still has consequences. For example, if you don't wear socks with your sneakers and you get sores on your heels, don't do your homework and get a bad grade, and choose to eat chips for breakfast only to be hungry again an hour later, you can only blame yourself. Not only will these poor choices create problems at that moment, but they also show your parents and other adults that you can't really handle the responsibility of taking care of yourself.

Think of it like this. Imagine you're doing a school project with one of your friends. The project instructions say in big red letters, "*This project MUST be printed out and stapled before it can be turned in.*" It's the Friday before the project's due date, so you and your friend spend the whole class putting together the finishing touches. Now all you have to do is print it out and staple it together, but the bell rings. Unfortunately, you don't have a printer at home, so your friend offers to use their printer over the weekend, promising to have it back on Monday morning. Fast forward to the following week. It's Monday morning, you see the clock strike 8:30 a.m., and the teacher tells everyone to turn in their projects. You look at your friend while they slowly say, "I forgot to print our project."

You gave your friend a chance to take responsibility for the first time with you, and they blew it. You probably won't trust that friend with more responsibilities after that, would you? Nope, not for a while! This situation is the same as your parents taking back some of the independence they've given you if you've shown you can't take your responsibilities seriously.

Here's the thing, you're only human, and humans make mistakes (yep, even adults). Sometimes you'll forget to do things that are your responsibility, and that's okay! Nobody expects you to be perfect as long as it doesn't become a habit. To prepare for these times, let's talk about a few fool-proof ways to win back your parents' trust, re-earn responsibilities, and eventually convince them to give you more independence:

Take Action!

There's no better way to prove that you can be responsible than by taking responsibility for things before anyone asks:

1. If the trashcan is full, tie it up and take it out. You can even put it in a new trash bag for bonus points!

2. When dinner is ready, set the table with silverware. Remember that forks go on the left side of the plate, and knives go on the right. I remember this rule with a small hack: 'fork' and 'left' both have four letters, and 'knife' and 'right' both have five letters.

3. If you see your room getting messy, go ahead and pick up things that aren't in their place.

If you haven't learned how to do some of these things, asking your family members to show you is also a great way to take action.

Chapter 1

FOOD FIRST: EASY COOKING HACKS YOU SHOULD KNOW

Did you know that Taylor Swift learned to cook when she was only a teen? At 16, Taylor released her first album, sang her own songs in front of crowds, and fell in love with cooking. Wait, what? Yep. It's true. While one of the biggest pop stars of all time was busy starting her career as a musician, she still set aside time to learn how to cook. Some people even say that learning to cook is the reason she became a famous singer... just kidding, but I'd make a bet to say that it at least helped her learn how to take care of herself.

Why Learning How to Cook Helps You Grow Up

Learning to cook is a super helpful step in building self-confidence and maturity, which are pretty important factors in becoming famous (and growing up.) Learning to cook is a lot more than just getting to make food when your body tells you you're hungry and there aren't any adults around to cook for you. While you must remember that some meals and cooking tools need a co-chef present, aka an adult, there are so many safe and easy meals you can make without help. When you're getting ready to whip up something tasty in the kitchen, you need to be prepared to feel confident in yourself to make quick decisions. These decisions can make the difference between your toast coming out golden brown or burnt to a crisp or your mac 'n cheese being perfectly creamy or runny and watery.

Don't worry too much if the first few tries aren't the best dishes you've ever had. Just like anything else, mastering cooking takes time and practice. Your confidence will grow the better you get, and before you know it, you'll be sitting down with your family while they all make "mmm" sounds eating the dinner you made all by yourself.

Speaking of making dinner all by yourself, when you're a kid, adults are in charge of making sure your stomach is full and happy. The fact that more than just the taste of the food is important isn't something that crosses your mind. Well, now that you're a tween and mature enough to learn how to cook, the time has come to learn that the *types* of food you eat are one of the most important parts of keeping your body healthy. This is where the maturity part comes in; not only does cooking involve decisions to make sure your food comes out tasting the way you plan, but it also involves making smart decisions about the ingredients in your food.

Yes, chocolate pancakes, cocoa puffs, and chocolate milk sound like a yummy breakfast, and when you're cooking your own food, you can technically choose to make chocolate breakfasts every morning. However, you're a mature tween, so you know that so much chocolate in the morning, every morning, will make your body very tired and unhappy by the afternoon. Instead of so much chocolate all at once, you can choose to replace the coco puffs with some eggs and drink a glass of iced water instead of chocolate milk. Remember, eating chocolate and other snack foods can still be done in a mature and healthy way. Just make sure you don't eat too much, too often.

Cooking Basics

When I was 11, my mom ran out to do last-minute Christmas shopping while my dad was at work. All I wanted to do was relax and enjoy my day watching TV when suddenly, my stomach started making those weird rumbling noises. There I was, alone and hungry for anything other than the celery sticks that seemed to be the only snack in the fridge. My mom would be back soon enough, and she could make me exactly what I wanted, a PB&J. But the time drug on. Five minutes, twelve minutes, twenty-six. My stomach got angrier, and I started feeling sick. I was about to give in and eat the celery sticks when my mom FINALLY walked through the door. She made me the sandwich, and I watched closely because I decided that I'd never live through that torture again. I was going to learn how to make my own food. How hard could it be anyway?

Many years later, I come to you with the answer to that question: it's not all that hard...most of the time anyway. Let's go through the most important cooking basics I started learning when I was your age.

Can You Read Recipes?

After a lot of trial and error, I've found that the easiest way to follow a recipe is a lot like how you solve a word problem on a math test: read all the instructions from beginning to end BEFORE you start cooking. This will save you a lot of time in the long run and make it less likely that you'll miss important steps. Cooking is pretty fast-paced, which can be stressful when you're just learning. I don't want you to feel anything other than excitement when you're learning to cook, so here's a tip: take some steps before the recipe guide says, "step one." I like to call these the "pre-steps for the non-professional chefs."

Pre-step one: Make sure you have everything the recipe needs. This includes opening boxes, tops, and anything else that holds the ingredient to make sure it isn't empty – or almost empty, been there, done that.

Pre-step two: Put every ingredient needed to make the meal right in front of you for easy grabbing.

PRO TIP: Use your pre-steps before starting any recipe so that your baking adventure ends with delicious success.

Pre-step three: Slowly re-read the recipe while chopping the vegetables and slicing the cheese.

After you finish the pre-steps, you're ready to follow the steps in your meal's recipe without feeling rushed. It's easiest to follow the steps closely if it's your first time making that specific meal, but recipes are fun because they can be changed to your liking. Everyone has different taste buds, which means there are tons of different ways to make the same meal. So after you've made something like the recipe says, you'll know if you'd like it better with more cheese and fewer onions or if you'd like it cooked for longer so it's a little crispier, or less time so it's softer. Next time, you can make these changes, and it'll be your very own recipe. Remember, even though the goal is to follow the recipe exactly at first, since there are so many different ways to make the same meal, you don't need to worry about getting it perfect. As long as you don't undercook the meat, burn the meal to ashes, or dump an entire package of salt into the ingredient mixture, those you're sharing the meal with probably won't even notice.

Easy Cooking Projects

It's time to let you in on some easy meals you can make as your first cooking project. A cool thing about cooking is that a lot of times, the meal that you can make in only a few minutes can look like it took a lot of time and effort. What's my favorite example of meals like this, you ask? Without a doubt, the answer is pasta: spaghetti, ravioli, linguine, penne, tortellini; you name it.

HOW TO MAKE PASTA

Pasta can be made with as little as three ingredients in only five to twelve minutes. You don't even need to pull out a cookbook to make it. Turn the box over, and it'll tell you everything you need to know.

1. Add the amount of water recommended into the pot.
2. Put the pot on the stove and turn the temperature to the highest setting.
3. Let the water come to a boil (that's when the pot is filled with lots of big bubbles).
4. Carefully dump in the pasta (you don't want boiling water to splash up and burn you).
5. Set the timer for the amount of time it says on the box.
6. After the time is up, pour out the water.
7. Add some butter.
8. Enjoy your solo-cooked meal!

Wait until you see the difference in the size of the pasta noodles before and after they're done – it's like magic.

How to Bake a Potato

Your self-cooked pasta is perfect, but it never hurts to have a side dish in case you're still hungry. There's never been a better, or easier to cook, side dish than a baked potato. If you have an hour to spare, preheat the oven to 400 degrees Fahrenheit, wrap your raw potato in tin foil, put it in an oven-safe pan, and pop it in. If you don't have an extra 60 minutes from cooking time to meal time, how does a microwave and 14 minutes for a fully baked potato sound? While your potato might not be quite as crispy, using a fork to poke holes in your plain potato and letting it spin in the microwave will result in a yummy baked potato in one-third of the time as the oven.

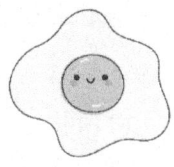

How to Boil an Egg

Not everyone is a pasta and baked potato for breakfast kind of person, so save that for later in the day and boil an egg instead. Two self-cooked meals in one day!? Now THAT'S what I call independence. I will admit that boiling an egg will take some practice before you get it perfect, but generally, it's easy to make it edible – as long as it doesn't crack before it's done. Add the eggs to a pot of cold water, put the pot on the stove, and let it boil for seven to ten minutes. The longer it cooks, the firmer the yolk (the yellow part) will be.

Baking Basics

Remember how I said that when you're cooking, people probably won't notice if you mess up an ingredient a little bit since there are so many different ways to make a meal? Well... unfortunately, that doesn't apply to baking. Even though baking and cooking have the whole making food thing in common, following the exact recipe when you're making something in the oven is crucial. If you have a sweet tooth for cake, brownies, pies, muffins, or anything sugary, consider learning how to follow recipe instructions your newest goal. Your measuring cups and spoons will be your new bestie.

My best advice when following any baking recipe ever is to:

1. Measure, measure, and measure again,
2. If it says to stir five times, don't even think about going for a sixth stir.
3. Be sure to keep sugar, flour, baking powder, and milk within reach at all times.
4. No matter what you do, don't forget to oil the pan.

Even though the room to mess up is very, very small in baking, the good news is that you can move slowly. So you have plenty of time to think, correct, and relax.

How to Operate the Oven

Operating the oven is the easiest step in baking, which is great because you'll be using it a LOT. Learning your way around the oven is one of those things that you only need to learn once before you're a pro. It takes an oven some time to warm up before it's ready to bake your desserts. It's important to read the recipe first so you can preheat the oven to the specific temperature in the recipe (I cannot stress this enough) while mixing and measuring. The oven is warm and ready when you hear a beeping sound.

While you don't have to worry about putting your dessert in the oven right when it beeps if it's not ready, it is very important to wait until that beep to put the dessert in and set the timer.

> **PRO TIP:** Set your timer the instant you put your treat in the oven. It's so easy to forget and accidentally leave your yummies in too long. How sad if they got burnt to a crisp!?

If you put something in the oven and set the timer before the beep, the oven won't be warm enough, and your dessert likely won't be fully cooked. Undercooked food of any kind doesn't just taste bad but can also be really dangerous to your health.

When you hear the beep and open the oven door to put your dessert pan inside, you'll notice multiple racks. The best choice for baking is the rack that is most in the middle of the oven.

If you aren't busy, turn on the oven light and watch your dessert bake. You'll be able to see your cookies get rounder, your cake rise, or your brownies get crispy. It's really cool! When your dessert is done baking, the timer you set when you put the treat in the oven will beep, which means the time has come to take it out. Go ahead and put your oven mitt on before you open the door. If you wait until after, it's easy to get so excited from the wonderful smell of fresh cookies and reach for the pan without the mitt, and this will definitely hurt badly enough to ruin the entire dessert... or so I've been told.

Safety & First Aid

The biggest reason you had to wait until you became a pre-teen to cook is that the kitchen can be dangerous if you're not careful. One of the best ways to prove to your parents that you're ready to learn to cook is by showing that you can be mature and responsible while handling food. Before touching any food item you plan to put in your mouth, you have to make sure you have clean, germ-free hands. Can you imagine germs from outside getting on your clean vegetables only because you didn't wash your hands? Gross! Speaking of germs, they LOVE raw meat, and these kinds of germs will make you SICK. If you're cooking anything with uncooked poultry or fish in the recipe, keep them separate from all other ingredients. After your hands or any cooking tool has touched the raw food, wash them really well with soap and water before letting them touch anything else. Even if it's just a drop of chicken juice on the cutting board or the knife – water, soap, and scrub before using those things for any other food. Raw food germs are ruthless. When your meal starts to come together, and the amazing smells fill the kitchen, it can be tempting to take a small taste. I know you're hungry and excited to try your meal, but the germs don't care. Even just a finger dip into a mixture with any raw food is enough for the germs to win and make you sick.

Sometimes, even when you take precautions, mistakes can happen while cooking. It happens to the best of us, so it's essential to have a first aid kit nearby. Make sure your kit is prepped with waterproof band-aids, cleansing wipes, and burn spray.

How to Clean the Kitchen

Have your parents ever put you in charge of washing the dishes after dinner? You've gathered the plates, silverware, and cups, grabbed the sponge, and scrubbed with soap and water. You even took the extra time to dry everything and put it all away in the cabinets and drawers. Ahh, there we go – a clean kitchen. *Sigh.*

I wish it could be that easy. While the dishes are clean, things are in their place, and you don't see any crumbs on the tables, there's still a lot to be done before you have a clean kitchen.

Taking on the responsibility of cooking can also mean cleaning the kitchen after you're done, so follow this checklist to make sure your kitchen not only *looks* clean but *is* clean.

- Re-soap your sponge, turn the water on, and scrub the sink. When cleaning the dishes, the sink is the first place the food and germs will stink, so this should be done after every meal.

- Take some sanitizing wipes and wipe down every inch and crevice of the counters, stove, and table to remove any grease, spills, or germs that escaped while you were cooking.

- Get a broom and sweep the whole kitchen, even the corners and places you definitely didn't have food. Don't forget to move the chairs and sweep the crumbs from under the table. To make things easy, sweep everything into a pile and push it into the broom pan before dumping it in the trash can.

- Speaking of the trash can, take the handles dangling on the sides of the bag and tie them into a bow. This will give you something to grab to lift the trash bag out of the trash can. Don't forget to put in a new bag! Throwing trash into a bagless trash can means reaching the bottom and taking it back out – eww.

- Put away any clutter on the counters – nothing makes a kitchen look dirty like random things laying out.

GET READY, GET SET, COOK!

Okay, let's do this. It's time to show yourself what you've learned and bake something sweet! Here is a step-by-step, easy to follow recipe to test out your cooking skills. Make sure to write in the notes section at the end of the recipe so you can see your progress for next time.

Very Chocolatey Cake

*Don't forget! Read the recipe twice and pre-step! *

Ingredients:
- 2 cups white sugar
- 1 ¾ cups all-purpose flour
- ¾ cup unsweetened cocoa powder
- 1 ½ teaspoons baking powder
- 1 ½ teaspoons baking soda
- 1 teaspoon salt
- 2 eggs
- 1 cup milk
- ½ cup vegetable oil
- 2 teaspoons vanilla extract
- 1 cup water
- Cooking spray
- 1 container of chocolate icing

Pre-step one: Get your measuring tools, a spoon, a 9x13 inch cake pan, and 2 mixing bowls.

Pre-step two: Head over to the pantry and grab all the ingredients you will need for this recipe. Get the milk and eggs out of the fridge, but don't forget to put them right back in the fridge as soon as you're done with them. Ever forgotten about the milk and left it out all night? Eww.

Pre-step three: Read through the entire recipe before you get started. It's always good to know what's coming. Don't worry if as you're making the cake you find yourself reading the recipe... rereading... reading again... and then going back yet again to double-check a measurement. You're not crazy. We all do it.

Step 1: Preheat the oven to 350° Fahrenheit.

Step 2: First we're going to mix up all the dry ingredients. The pros mix up all the dry ingredients, mix up all the wet ingredients, then mix the two groups together. They say that this is so everything gets mixed evenly. So, measure out all the dry ingredients (sugar, flour, cocoa powder, baking powder, baking soda, and salt) and mix them together in the bowl.

> **PRO TIP:** Crack your eggs in a separate bowl. That way if you get some shell in it, you can easily see to scoop it out. No tricky eggshell bits are going to sneak past you!

Step 3: Now it's time for the wet ingredients. Measure and mix in all the other wet ingredients (eggs, milk, vegetable oil, vanilla extract, and water).

Step 4: Pour the wet ingredients into the bowl with the dry ingredients and mix them together just until they are combined. You'll know it's ready when you can see that all the dry ingredients are wet. Ta-da! You now have cake batter!

Step 5: Spray the bottom and sides of your cake pan so that after your cake is baked it won't stick to your pan. Then all your cake batter goes into the pan.

Step 6: Put on your oven mitts and put the cake pan in the oven. Be careful. The oven is super hot.

Step 7: Let your cake bake for 35 minutes, and watch it rise!

Step 8: Put your oven mitts on again, open the oven door, and carefully take out the pan.

Step 9: At this point, the cake is probably done baking. But how do you know for sure? It may look baked on the outside, but how do you know if the inside is done without taking a huge scoop out of the middle? Here's a trick. Take a toothpick (or a knife if you can't find a toothpick), stick it directly in the middle of the cake, and then pull it back out. How does it look? If it has little bits of uncooked batter on it, put the cake back in for a few more minutes, then do that test again. It if came out clean, congratulations! You just baked your first cake!

Step 10: Let the cake cool for twenty minutes then go crazy with the icing!

Sweet!

How'd it go?

Notes _____

_____

_____

_____

_____

_____

Motivation Moment

You don't need to look like a professional chef your first, second, or even twentieth time cooking. Truthfully, my first solo-cooked meal was awful! However, it didn't stop me from getting back up and trying again and again...and again. The most important things to focus on when getting ready to learn how to cook are to be prepared, focused, and responsible. A lot of things can go wrong in the kitchen, from small things like misreading the recipe and forgetting to use a cutting board (RIP to the counters) to big things like grabbing the wrong end of a knife, forgetting to put on your oven mitts when taking out your cake, and reusing the unwashed kitchen tools after they touched raw meat. Even though it seems like a lot of information to remember, I promise it'll come a lot more naturally than you think – and if it doesn't, well, practice makes perfect! Never forget that learning to cook is about having fun while helping you learn new things. The best part? Cooking is only the beginning of what you'll learn as you grow and mature through your tween years.

Chapter 2

SPICK AND SPAN: DOING CHORES WHILE STILL HAVING FUN

"Chores." Something about the word just *sounds* boring. When people say it, they don't seem happy or excited. In fact, they make chores seem kind of horrible. So, when you're told that as a tween, it's time to start taking responsibility for doing chores, it can seem like one of the worst parts of growing up. Since people make it *sound* like it's no fun, it makes your brain *think* it's no fun. Have you ever heard someone say, "never judge a book by its cover"? It's one of those popular sayings that adults say when something looks bad but ends up being great. The boring-looking word "chores" happens to be one of those things you can't judge by how it looks or sounds because they're the exact opposite of boring and horrible. The only reason some people think chores aren't fun is that they haven't learned the right way to do them or all the great things they can do for you! Learning how to do chores doesn't just help out your family, which is already a great perk, but they have been proven to help you do better in school, make friends easier, and feel happier.

Cleaning

Cleaning is at the very top of every chore list, but would it surprise you to know that a lot of people don't know how to do it correctly? Yep! Believe it or not, many people think that if something looks clean, it must be clean, but that's not true. Think of it like this: Imagine you drop your cheese stick on the ground outside. You pick it up to throw it away and notice that you can't see any dirt on it. Would you still eat? Probably not! You know that even though you can't see the dirt, it's definitely there. The same thing is true inside your house. Just because things are put away, and you don't actually see dirt on the floor, doesn't mean it can't use a thorough cleaning session. So, let's learn how to clean so well that you could drop your cheese stick on the floor and still be able to pick it up and eat it.

PS, just because you can doesn't mean you should.

PPS, please don't eat anything you drop on the floor... ever.

The living room is where you, your family, your friends, and your family's friends all come to talk, relax, and, honestly, watch TV. Since so much happens in the living room, it will probably always look a little "lived-in." No matter how often your parents re-fluff the couch pillows, straighten the rug, and re-fold the blankets, it's not long before they're all messed up again. However, there's a difference between a little messy and straight-up dirty. Go ahead and look around the living room. Do you see anything that shouldn't be there? Maybe your bookbag lying next to the couch, some mail your parents still need to go through, or trash from your afternoon snack? Whatever it is, put it up or throw it away. This is where most people will say, "Alright! Looks good; cleaning is complete." Not you, though; you know there's a lot more to do. Instead, you're going to take out an old rag and get to dusting.

Dusting is cool because you get to see a difference super fast. Just spray and wipe, and suddenly the lamp, table, picture frames, or whatever piece of furniture that was covered in grey dust dots is all shiny. Check out the rag you used to dust and see how much dirt and dust came off! Now that the dust is gone, you can move on to the windows. You really never notice how smudge-y windows get until after you've cleaned them. They get fingerprints, animal nose prints (or your nose prints), and little dirt specs you usually overlook until after you've sprayed it with glass spray and wiped everything away with paper towels. Wait until you see freshly cleaned windows – they're so see-through that you almost forget you're looking through glass. Now everything is mostly clean... except for the floor. While you were dusting and wiping, some of the dust and dirt definitely fell onto the floor, which is why it's always smart to save vacuuming for last. I've always liked vacuuming – it's fun to vacuum in super straight lines on the carpet and rugs so you can see the pattern it makes. When it's time, get the vacuum, turn it on, and make your own pattern! Don't get too carried away and forget to go over all the spots. When you're all done, step back and admire your complete cleaning work. Take in a big whiff – you'll even be able to smell the clean.

> **PRO TIP:** Clean smarter, not harder. Save vacuuming for last so that you can suck up any sneaky dust bunnies that fell on the floor when you were dusting.

Okay, so your living room looks clean just by picking up things that don't belong, but that is NOT the case for your bathroom. Take a moment to say a quick "thank you" to your bathroom. It really takes the trophy for the dirtiest room in the house, and you can tell. The shower washes away the dirt and sweat after a long day of school, the sink rinses down the food and germs from your teeth every morning and night, and the toilet...well... you know what the toilet does. It doesn't take long for almost every inch of your bathroom to get dirty, so it's important to know how to get it nice and clean, at least until your next shower. To start, you can follow the same routine as cleaning the living room. Put things in their place, do some dusting, and instead of wiping down the window, use the glass cleaner and paper towels to wipe the mirror, and vacuum the floor. Easy part: done.

Now, prepare to get your hands dirty! As someone who doesn't love getting their hands dirty, I recommend getting some waterproof, reusable, cleaning gloves before diving hands first into the toilet, but that's totally up to you – hands can always be washed. I'm actually being a little bit dramatic. Before even starting the hands-to-toilet action, you'll be using a toilet brush to clean off the dirtiest part: the rim. Use your toilet bowl cleaner to squirt under the rim of the toilet and watch it drip down the bowl for five whole minutes. Then, grab the toilet brush and scrub every inch where the cleaner went. Just a tip: try not to look at the dirt coming out from under the rim – save yourself and just flush the toilet. Next, get your all-purpose spray cleaner and spray it under the seat's lid, on the lid, and all over the entire outside of the toilet. Use your old sponge specifically for toilet cleaning and toilet cleaning only, and wipe it clean.

Okay! The worst part is over. Let's move on to the second dirtiest spot in the bathroom: the bathtub/shower. My favorite way to clean the shower is by leaving all-purpose spray in there along with an old sponge (not the one used to clean the toilet) and using my shower time to also quickly clean it. I've found that doing this makes sure that my shower never has the chance to get dirty. While combining shower time with shower cleaning time works well for me, it doesn't mean it works for everyone. You can always just clean your shower separately (like most people). Just spray the all-purpose cleaner all over the tub or shower, get an old rag (again, not the rag you use to clean your toilet), and scrub away. Make sure to rinse every place you sprayed when you're done scrubbing. Perfect – to the sink! Make sure the drain is completely closed in the sink bowl, spray it with an all-purpose cleaner, and turn the water on. Let it fill up with warm water while you spray the countertops with, once again, an all-purpose cleaner. I guess that's why they call it all-purpose; you really can use it everywhere. Once the sink is full, wet an old rag and wipe every part of the sink you sprayed. Let the water in the sink drain and wipe the bowl with the rag.

There you go, squeaky clean! Time to move on to the most important room of all...

Your bedroom is YOUR special place. You spend at least eight hours in it every night. It's decorated with your things, and it represents who you are. You get to come here, close the door, and relax without anyone around. But... trying to relax with a huge mess around you can be just the opposite of relaxing. You've practiced dusting, wiping, scrubbing, and vacuuming in the other rooms, so show your bedroom those skills by giving it the grand, professional cleaning treatment. After that is done, all that's left is the bed. Take off the sheets you've slept on all week and throw them in the laundry bin (we'll talk about that soon). Get a clean pair of sheets and pillowcases – things are about to get intense.

Before you start, know that nobody – literally not one person – is good at what you're about to do. This is the part of the sheet-changing process that makes even professionals go crazy and the true definition of the sheets vs. human challenge: the fitted sheet. The fitted seat is the one that is bunched together by elastic at each corner. Lay it out on your bed with the longest part going from the top of the bed to the bottom. Now, it's time. Ready for battle? Take the top left corner of the sheet and fit it over the top left corner of the mattress; simple enough, right? Now, walk around to the right side of the bed, take the top right corner of the sheet, and fit it over the top right corner of the mattress. Easy? Wait for it – here it comes. Walk down to the bottom right corner of the bed, take the bottom right corner of the sheet, and fit it over the mattress. One of the top corners popped off, didn't it? Now, do you see what I mean by sheets vs. human challenge? Don't worry; you'll win. It's just going to take a few times of re-putting each corner back over the mattress before all four corners finally stay put.

Success, you've now defeated the fitted sheet. Your prize is the regular ole' top sheet. Line up the long end of the sheet with the long end of the bed (head to foot) and the short end of the sheet to the short end of the bed (right to left). Now, all that's left are the pillowcases. Take the open end of the pillowcase and put it over the short end of the pillow. Push enough of the pillow into the pillowcase so it doesn't fall out when you pick it up. Grab the open ends of the pillowcase with part of the pillow inside and hold it while you jump up and down until the end of the pillow has reached the closed end of the pillowcase. Now throw the pillow onto the bed, lay down, and take a nap because that was a FULL workout.

SPICK AND SPAN: DOING CHORES WHILE STILL HAVING FUN

Laundry

See? Told you we'd get back to the laundry bin soon. You've probably noticed that you always have clean clothes to wear, but have you ever wondered exactly how they go from smelly, dirty, and in the laundry bin, to clean and hanging in the closet? Well, there's a whole process that your parents go through to make that happen. The most important step to take when washing laundry is separating everything into categories of color and material. To keep things simple, follow this guide:

Step 1: Material –

- Delicates, sheets, and towels in one pile.
- All other material in another pile.

Step 2: Colors –

- Lights alone in one pile: baby pink, light purple, baby blue, light green, etc.
- Darks alone in one pile: black, grey, brown, navy, red, etc.
- Whites alone in one pile: white and white only.

Step 3: Each pile is one separate load of laundry. Make sure to pay attention to the water temperature setting that the washing machine will use to wash each pile.

- COLD water = delicates, sheets, towels, and darks
- WARM water = lights
- HOT water = whites

Step 4: Add in the laundry detergent. Read the instructions on the back of the bottle or box to know how much to pour over each separate load of laundry. A little goes a long way! If you're washing your pile of whites, add bleach to make them look brand new (be careful not to get bleach on your skin).

Let your washing machine do what it does best, and you'll come out with clean clothes ready to be dried. When using the dryer, never put in anything that you wouldn't mind getting a little smaller. Since dryers get very hot, they can shrink your clothes! If you want to be sure nothing gets shrunk, lay everything out on a drying rack with enough space that they don't touch so they can air dry. Laundry 101 is complete, but...

EMERGENCY! You've spilled spaghetti sauce all over your favorite shirt, and now it's ruined. Red sauce on a white shirt? It's done for; there's no way you can ever wear it again. Wait! Not so fast – it's just a stain, and I'm going to teach you how to save your shirt from the trash can. When you notice the spill, carefully change your shirt, and take it to the sink to be treated. The quicker you notice the stain, the easier it'll be to get it out. Make sure to look at the tag on the back of the shirt. Unless it says, "dry clean only" (this will usually be silk and wool materials), we're good to go.

Step 1: Turn the shirt inside out. We're going to be working from the back of the material.

Step 2: Turn on the sink and let cool water run over your shirt for about a minute.

Step 3: Pick up your shirt, squeeze the extra water, and lay it flat.

Step 4: Put a little bit of laundry detergent directly on the stain. If it's a big stain, carefully rub it with a soft brush or your finger; if it's a small stain, don't touch it.

Step 5: Rinse your shirt in the sink with cool water once again until there are no more soap bubbles.

Step 6: Squeeze out the extra water and lay your shirt back down before getting a sponge or bunched-up paper towels to dab the stain with white vinegar.

Step 7: Rinse the vinegar and repeat steps five and six until the stain is either gone or very light.

Step 8: Spray the stain with a stain remover if you have it, toss it in the washing machine, set the water to cold, and let it wash as usual.

Your shirt should come out looking brand new!

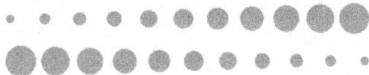

Congratulations for coming this far and welcome to level three of doing laundry: ironing. When I was your age, I had an experience with the iron that I'd like to make sure you don't repeat. Let me tell you the story... I got a fancy pink dress specifically to wear to school on my birthday, but I decided to throw it on the floor when I got it home instead of hanging it up like I should have (which would have solved all my problems). It stayed on the floor for about a week, getting all wrinkled and crinkled, but I didn't think anything of it... until I put it on. I could see that it was unwearable the way it was, but ironing it couldn't be too hard, right? Well, maybe it wouldn't have been if I had read a book like you and known what I was doing. I took out the iron and laid the dress on the ironing board. Good first step. I then put the iron on top of the dress, which immediately burned a hole in the middle. As you can guess, I didn't get to wear my birthday dress.

That being said, now I know it's very important to know the material of the clothing you're ironing because the material completely determines the temperature you choose to set your iron. Your clothes' material type will be written on their tags. So take a look at this guide so you never end up burning a hole through your birthday outfit:

- Acetate, 290 F.
- Acrylic or Nylon, 275 F.
- Cotton, 400 F.
- Linen, 445 F.
- Polyester, Silk, or Wool, 300 F.
- Rayon, 375 F.
- Triacetate, 390 F.

Okay, now you're ready to iron.

Step 1: Set your iron board in a safe, open space and lay your clothing on it, making sure it's completely flat.

Step 2: There's a hole in the top of your iron. Fill it to the top with water. This will make steam while you iron, making ironing easier.

Step 3: Plug in your iron and turn the dial to the correct heat setting for the material of your piece of clothing. Look back at the chart if you need a reminder of which temperature to use.

Step 4: After giving the iron about 30 seconds to heat up, put it directly on the clothes and slowly and carefully slide it across the material. If any wrinkles appear while you're ironing, put the iron down, flatten the wrinkle, and then continue.

Step 5: Turn the piece of clothing over on its other side and repeat until it's wrinkle-free!

Please, please, please don't ever let the iron sit in one spot while you're ironing. Instead, make sure you're sliding the iron around the shirt at all times. Letting the iron stay in one place on your clothes will not only cause you to relive my birthday dress mess, but it could even start a fire.

> **PRO TIP:** If you don't have an iron, dampen your wrinkly shirt with a little bit of water and throw it in the dryer with a dry towel or two for 10 minutes. It won't do as good of a job as the iron, but it's easy!

Caring for Pets and Plants

Your pets give you all that they can. Love, comfort, entertainment, cuddles – they're the best. Whether you have a dog, cat, lizard, fish, hamster, or any other animal, your pet has all sorts of different things they need to live a happy life. However, since your pet doesn't have opposable thumbs to open food containers, let themselves out to go to the bathroom, and aren't tall enough to reach the sink to refill their water bowl, they rely on you entirely. You can forget to wash the dishes, make your bed, or vacuum the floor sometimes without anything terrible happening, but you absolutely cannot forget to take care of your pet, even for a day. Making sure your pet has clean water, healthy food to eat, and a place to use the bathroom are the most basic chores of having a pet, but it's important to give up some of your TV or phone time to give them attention and exercise every single day.

EPIC BOOK OF KID LIFE SKILLS

Do you know anything else that might be living in your house that needs you to stay alive? They're usually green and leafy and make the air cleaner. Yep, plants! Plants are like 10 levels down from pets when it comes to responsibility, but it's still important to know their different needs. Plants only need three things to survive: water, light, and food. However, you HAVE to know the type of plant you have to keep them healthy and happy because some plants can be super picky. Unlike pets, you don't need to worry about watering your plant daily. Overwatering is actually the most common way people accidentally kill their plants, so forgetting a watering day isn't too big of a deal. Plants almost always come with instructions, so be sure to follow them, but you can add them to your weekly chore chart for most plants. Simply check the top two inches of soil with your finger to make sure it isn't completely dry. If it is, give it some water; if it isn't, leave it be. After that, put it by the window to get some sunshine, and you should have a happy plant!

Cleaning the Car

Put your bathing suit on; you're getting soaked! Cleaning the car is probably the most fun chore because there's no way you won't get covered in bubbles and water. Start professionally and prepare the bucket, soap, hose, and cleaning brush. Pour a few drops of soap into the bucket and fill it with water so it looks like a mini bubble bath. Grab your brush and give it a big dip in the bucket; you're starting with the tires. Scrub every tire like you would if you got marker on the kitchen table and had to get it off before your mom gets home from the store – hard! After every tire is scrubbed down, turn on your hose, and rinse all the suds off really well before dumping out the whole bucket of water and soap. It's important to rinse the bucket before adding new drops of soap and refilling it with water - you don't want the dirt from your tires getting on the rest of the car. Nice! Now you're going to split up the car into seven sections. No, not physically split it up, just in your mind. You want to wash cars in small sections because with the sun shining, soap dries *fast* and dried soap all over the car will make it look even dirtier than before all of that washing. Get a soft, large sponge, dunk it in your bucket of soap and water and wash each of your sections separately. Rinse each of them with your hose before starting a new section. Your sections are:

1. The front right side door
2. The back right side door
3. The front left side door
4. The back left side door
5. The hood (front)
6. The tail (back)
7. The roof

Make sure to do the roof section first, but all other sections can be washed in any order you want. Now that the car is sparkly clean and shiny with water take a microfiber towel and dry it in the same sections you washed.

Stand back and check it out! Who wouldn't want to be picked up from school in that?

How to Make Chores Joyful

When people don't like chores, it's because they don't know how to make them fun. I want you to enjoy chores, so try these ideas on your next chore day!

1. **Crank up your favorite playlist:** You can make a playlist specifically for chores to help you dance and sing your way through the entire chore list.

2. **Write down what you want to accomplish first:** Putting a check next to each chore that I finish is one of my favorite things to do. Every check mark that I write gives me the motivation to keep going! Use colored pencils or crayons to make colorful check marks if you want to make it even better.

3. **Ask your parents for some cuter cleaning tools:** Cleaning tools come in SO many colors, and who doesn't want to use things with their favorite colors and fun designs? Ask your parents if you can pick out your own sponges, wipes, broom, and bucket so your cleaning tools can be cuter!

4. **Watch a movie:** Once you get some practice, cleaning is like riding a bike. You don't need to put much thought into each step because your hands already know what to do, so put a new movie on the TV to take your mind off the dust rag!

5. **Turn it into a game:** Making up games to go with your chores is super easy. You can time yourself each time you start a new chore and try to go faster (while still doing a good job) than the last time you did that chore. You can include your friends or family and compete to see who does the best cleaning job, or you can ask your parents to make a cleaning scavenger hunt so you can be on the hunt for different things you can only find while cleaning.

Prove Your Progress!

Activity

Your biggest goals in learning to do chores are to have fun and grow your independence, but... it would be nice to also find a way to show your parents all of the progress you've made, wouldn't it? Parents have busy lives, and sometimes they forget to really pay attention to the small details around them, so it's not hard for them to take a bit longer than you'd like them to notice when you've done some extra chores around the house. Don't worry! I've got you covered. You're going to make a chore chart – time to get crafty.

You'll need: paper, crayons or colored pencils, scissors, and some sticky magnets.

Step 1: Using this page, write a list of all the chores you can do or want to learn to do.

1. _____ 6. _____
2. _____ 7. _____
3. _____ 8. _____
4. _____ 9. _____
5. _____ 10. _____

Step 2: With the list of chores you made above, draw a picture that reminds you of each chore. For example: Laundry = a picture of a shirt, dusting = a picture of a rag, and taking care of pets = a picture of a dog.

Step 3: Write the words: 'Start' and 'Finished' in big letters at the bottom of the page with your pictures.

Step 4: Use your scissors to cut out each picture. Cut out 'Start' and 'Finished' into two pieces.

Step 5: Put one sticky magnet on the back of every picture and both words.

Step 6: Gather your chore magnet and take them with you to your fridge.

Step 7: Choose one side of the fridge to put your chore chart magnets. Put 'Start' on the left and 'Finished' on the right, and stick each chore picture you need to do under the 'Start' magnet and everything you've already done under the 'Finished' magnet.

Awesome! Now you and your parents will see your chore chart with all the chores you've finished every day. Problem: solved.

Motivation Moment

How do you feel after reading all the steps to learning how to do chores? Would you be able to do it all perfectly in one day the first time you try? If you said yes, you should apply for the world record for cleaning because that is some real talent! To be truthful, just like anything else, doing chores takes practice, so you won't get it all done perfectly, super-fast and fun for at least a few tries. But, I promise you one hundred percent will get there. Want to know how I know you will? A long time ago, a very famous author named Helen Keller grew up without being able to see or hear. Life was more complicated for Helen since she had to learn how to live differently than most people, but she didn't let that stop her. By only five years old, Helen had already learned how to do chores all by herself! How impressive is that? If Helen Keller could do it, you can too! Sometimes you may forget to pick up picture frames before dusting, accidentally use your toilet sponge to clean the sink, wash your darks on hot, or clean a second section of the car before rinsing the first section. While mistakes might add some time to your chores since you'll have to redo them, they don't take away from having fun and feeling proud when you're done. However, it's a good idea to at least try to finish your chores quickly. You know what the adults say, "time is money"...

Chapter 3

MONEY MATTERS: HOW TO SECURE THE BAG

How much do you know about money? Sure, you probably learned how to count coins and dollars in your first years of elementary school, but do you really know how it works? If you said yes, then you're ahead of the game! So many people your age and into their teens have never even heard of money terms like budget, interest, expenses, and income. I know you aren't quite at the age where you feel like knowing those fancy terms is all that important, but trust me when I say that learning early will make things WAY easier in the long run. As a matter of fact, a group of teens in North Carolina are so sure that knowledge of money is important for young people they started an entire business to help their peers learn the basics of money management.

Why It's a Good Idea to Save

I'm going to be completely real with you. It doesn't matter how old you get; deciding to put money away for another time instead of using it to buy something you want now will probably never be what you *want* to do. However, making the mature choice to take at least some of the money you make and save it will make future you very, very happy. I know it's hard to imagine yourself at any age beyond maybe next year, so think of it like this: It's your birthday. Your parents give you a crisp $100 bill and tell you to spend it however you want. So you shop around and get a few cool things, take them to the cashier, and pay a total of $87. Cool! You're happy with your new stuff... until the next day when you find out the latest video game you've been waiting for finally came out. It's $60, but since you spent most of your money on random toys yesterday, you only have $13. If only you had saved your money for just a little while, you could buy the game. But, since you chose not to, you have to wait, and who knows when the next time will be that you'll have that much money again. Things like this happen all the time when you're an adult, but instead of not having the money for something you want, like a video game, it'll be something you need, like a car.

How to Save

So, you agree that saving is a good idea, but how do you start? Sadly, most schools don't have a class on money management and saving 101, but don't worry! I'll teach you all you need to know. You might think, "I don't even have any money; I'm too young to work." That's fine! It's never too early to learn, and it's never too early to ask your parents to open a savings account for you, even if you don't have any savings yet. Having a savings account ready for you will make it a lot easier to actually save your money when you do get some because keeping money just lying around makes it very tempting to spend. A savings account is an account with a bank that keeps your money safe. They even reward you for leaving the savings in the account by adding small amounts of money to what you already have, called interest. You'll definitely want to keep adding more to your savings whenever you can because the more money you have in your savings account, the more interest that money earns. Yep! You earn money by literally doing nothing at all. Putting any of your money into your savings account is already great, but to really see your savings grow, it's best to set a goal for yourself. Goals are cool because they give you a reason to keep track of the amount of money you have and the motivation to keep saving. Say your goal is to have $20 in savings. You put $10 that you got from your grandparents, $2 from when dad gave you ice cream money but couldn't find the kind you like, and $1 from the quarters you found while cleaning under the couch. When you add that up, that's $13, and if your goal is $20, you can see that you only need to add $7 more! I know what you're thinking; saving must mean you have to do math. Yes, a little bit of math is involved, but I promise it's worth it.

PRO TIP: Make a fun container to store your savings in while you're waiting to take them to the bank. Find an empty box from the pantry and decorate it with stickers and your own drawings!

While making a goal for your savings, you might as well go ahead and start a budget too. A budget is an amount of money for something that you can't go over without giving up something else. For example, your budget for school lunches is $10 per week. You go to school for five days every week, so you can spend $2 on lunch every day without running out of money. However, on Thursday, you decide to buy a brownie for dessert that was 50 cents, along with your $2.00 lunch, making your total for Thursday $2.50.

Now, you've spent:

    $2.00 on Monday

    $2.00 on Tuesday

    $2.00 on Wednesday

    $2.50 on Thursday

When you add that together, it comes out to a total of $8.50. No problem, but... you still have one more day of school this week, Friday, and you've spent $8.50 of your $10.00 budget, which only leaves you with $1.50. Oh no. Since you bought the brownie on Thursday, you're 50 cents short on the $2.00 you need to pay for lunch, and now you have to be hungry for the rest of the school day. Having to be hungry for several hours is NO fun, even if it is for only one day, which is why knowing how to budget and sticking to that budget is so important!

I have a secret for you, money math doesn't always need to be done in your head, not even a little bit. There are apps that you or your parents can download on a cell phone that are specifically made to help you manage money. These apps can do all sorts of things, like telling you how much you *can* spend and *should* spend, keeping track of everything you buy, splitting your money into different categories, and always making sure you know just how much money you have left. No excuse to not budget your money now, huh? Making your own budget makes it super easy to plan ahead. When you're walking around a store with some dollars in your pocket and no specific plans of when to spend them, making the mistake of buying something silly is SO easy. Those dollars have nowhere to be, so why not get a new bag of pens just because they're blue and the ones at home are black? Sure, that may sound like a good purchase, but I bet you won't be too thrilled when you have to cancel movie plans with your friend because you spent your money on pens and can't afford a ticket. Budgeting gives every dollar you have a specific use, so next time you're in the store with cash in your pocket and you see something cool, you'll know that money already has other plans.

Show Off Your Savings!

Activity

Saving is hard. It takes a lot of maturity and self-discipline, especially when you don't even know what future you will do with all the money you're saving for later. When is later? What is later? When do you finally see your hard work of saving for so long pay off?

Well, now is when you decide! Close your eyes and picture the thing you want most in the world. Don't hold back; this is your dream, so don't just say a bag of chips you saw at the gas station earlier. What do you see? A bike, a dog, an Xbox, a trampoline, whatever it is, write it down below.

The thing I want most in the world is _____.

Done? Okay. Now, get on the computer, or ask your parents to Google the price of the thing you want most in the world and write it below

This will cost $ _____.

There you go! The number you just wrote down is your new savings goal. Try not to take any money out of your savings account until it reaches the goal. Knowing that you're saving towards something you want will motivate you to save instead of spend.

Hint: If you didn't pay much attention to the section above on budgeting, this is your chance to go back and re-read it. You may or may not be making your own very soon...

How to Be a Smart Spender

Everyone knows how to spend money, but only some know how to spend money wisely. Learning how to be smart with spending your money is a skill that's definitely worth mastering, but there are some rules you'll have to follow.

Rule #1: Don't be influenced! Falling into the trend trap is one of the fastest and easiest ways to burn through your money. I get it, believe me. It's not exactly easy to see your friends playing with their Nintendo Switch, wearing tie-dye sweatshirts, and taking selfies on polaroid cameras, all while choosing to *not* buy them for yourself. Trends come and go, so making sure you actually want the thing you're feeling influenced to buy will be super important in lessening the chances of getting something called "buyer's remorse." Let's say you get an expensive new bright orange bookbag at the beginning of the school year because everyone else did. Joining the trend feels great for a while, but you're not going to be so happy when you have to keep using it when it's no longer trendy, and you remember that you actually hate the color orange. THAT'S buyer's remorse. I'm not saying you should never participate in the trends; it doesn't have to be that dramatic. However, before you buy something, step back and ask yourself, "Do I actually like this, or do I only want it because everyone else thinks it's cool?" This one question will make sure you'll always be happy with your purchase and save you a *whole lot* of money. Easy. You're mature, self-disciplined, and responsible with money; influence won't get to you. Level one: complete. Level two is when things get harder.

Rule #2: Be extra mindful when going shopping with your friends. No one can convince you that you want something you don't really want, quite like your friends. When you combine being at the store with their influence and money in your pocket, remembering to ask that one important question might just slip your mind. Your friends aren't trying to make you buy something just so you'll regret it, but it's easy to get carried away because you're all having fun. However, it's a lot less dangerous to your wallet to go shopping without them. This brings us to...

> **PRO TIP:** If you aren't sure if you really want something or it's just an impulse buy, sleep on it! If you wake up the next morning and decide it wouldn't actually be that cool, way to go. You didn't waste your money. But if you still want it the next day, go for it!

Rule #3: Go shopping with your parents. It's a safe bet that your parents likely aren't following the trends like you are, so you don't have to worry about them falling for the trend trap and convincing you to buy something you've never talked about wanting before. As a matter of fact, it's a lot more likely that they'll talk you out of buying a lot of things and hold you accountable for following the fourth rule of smart spending...

Rule #4: Research expensive things before buying. This is the rule I've been a victim of in the past, possibly more than a few times... and I blame social media. Tiktok and Instagram are GREAT at making you buy things you don't need without much thinking. Some things seem super cool and useful in pictures and videos, but when you get it in the mail and actually start using it, you quickly realize that it isn't all that useful, and you probably should have at least researched enough to read the reviews before clicking 'buy.' When I say "you" here, I completely mean me. Don't be like me. Make sure to do some Googling and review reading before spending your hard-earned money on something that ends up being a big waste. Honestly, just leave the things you see on Instagram and TikTok out of your budget entirely.

Activity

Budget Your Bucks!

Okay, fine. You can have a second chance. Go back and re-read the section on budgeting but for real this time! Even if you've already downloaded your budgeting app, it's super important to learn how to do it on your own too. It's time to create your budget:

Step 1: Write down your monthly income. This includes your allowance, holiday presents, sneaky cash from grandma, or any other way you make money.

Step 2: Make a list of things you want. These are mainly small things, like dessert after lunch, movie tickets, and school game entrance fees. And yes, those trendy shoes. In your list, be sure to write down the price of each thing. Then, add up the total of those things and write them at the bottom of the list.

Total Income: $_____

Needs Price

1. $

2. $

3. $

4. $

5. $

6. $

7. $

8. $

9. $

10. $

Total: $

Step 3: Next, write down a list of things you need and their prices. These are things like your school lunch, cleats for soccer practice, school supplies, etc. Add up the total of those things and write them at the bottom of the list.

Total Income: $_____

Wants Price

1. $

2. $

3. $

4. $

5. $

6. $

7. $

8. $

9. $

10. $

Total: $

Step 4: Since your wants and needs are all added up, you can now find out the percentages of your income that will go into three categories: Needs, Wants, and Savings. I recommend the classic

50/30/20 budgeting rule. It means that 50% of your income goes to the things you need category, 30% of your income goes towards the thing you want category, and 20% goes to your savings account.

Let's say you have a monthly income of $100. By using the 50/30/20 budgeting rule, you calculate that:

Needs: 50% of $100 = $50

Wants: 30% of $100 = $30

Savings: 20% of $100 = $20

So, each month, you have $50 to spend on things you need, $30 to spend on things you want, and $20 goes into your savings account.

Type this formula into your calculator to find out the amount of money you can have in all three categories when using 50/30/20.

Needs: 0.5 X (total income) = $_____

Wants: 0.3 X (total income) = $_____

Savings: 0.2 X (total income) = $_____

How to Earn More Money

You may have run into a small problem when calculating the amount of money you can spend in your three categories: you don't quite have enough to cover the total of everything on your list! Before you start crossing things off from the Wants category (yes, sadly, those are the first to go), you can find ways to add more money to your monthly income. Heads up, most of these will need a little help from your parents, but here are some of my favorites:

Sell Used Items Online – Make sure to ask for your parent's permission, but if you have old clothes or shoes that don't fit anymore or toys that you don't want but are in good shape, don't throw them out! There are a bunch of different websites online where you can list them for sale and make some extra cash.

Yard Services – Have you ever helped your parents take care of your yard? You know, things like mowing grass, pulling weeds, planting flowers, and raking leaves? There are a lot of people who either don't have the time, don't enjoy it, or can't do those kinds of yard work that will pay you to do it for them!

Pet Sitting & Dog Walking – So many adults have to leave their pups at home while they go to work every day. They'll be super happy to pay you a small fee to walk their dogs while they're away.

Sell Your Crafts – 'DIY' videos are all over the internet, and a lot of them are really easy to do! Find a video showing how to make a craft you like, make a quick trip to the Dollar Store, and get creative! You can sell your finished products for much more than it takes to make them.

Motivation Moment

If I haven't succeeded in making you believe that money management and smart spending skills are important yet, maybe Emma Watson will (you know, Hermione from *Harry Potter* and Bell from *Beauty and the Beast*.) Emma is a SUPER famous actress, and she's also SUPER good about following the rules of smart spending. As a teen, Emma took a class to learn all about saving, budgeting, and sustainable spending, and she still keeps up with everything she's learned. I don't know about you, but I'll be following the lead of the woman who's worth $85 million and working on my budgeting and saving skills! Even though you might not make multi-millions like Emma Watson, there are still so many ways to earn more money to add to your income and increase your savings. If you decide to try out any of the extra earning ideas I've mentioned, make sure to tell a trusted adult, *especially* if you're selling to strangers.

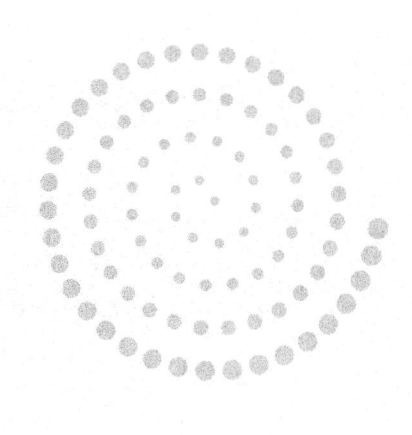

Chapter 4

MORE THAN STRANGER DANGER: LEARNING THE ROPES OF PERSONAL SAFETY

Snapchat, Instagram, TikTok, YouTube, Twitter, Facebook, Reddit, Pinterest, Discord, what am I forgetting? It's hard to even keep up with all the social media and instant messaging sites these days because there are so many! They're pretty great when it comes to talking to your friends and staying in the loop of what people are doing, how they're feeling, where they're going, what they're wearing, basically anything you'd want them to know… and sometimes maybe a *little* more than you want to know. Can you imagine how strange it would be if someone you don't know randomly walked up and started telling you all the personal details about their life before even saying hello? Somehow, though, it feels totally normal to do that online. I mean, that's what everyone does, so why shouldn't you do it too? There's something about being online that doesn't exactly feel like real life, so it's easy to forget that the things you're sharing, saying, and doing *are* actually real and *will* affect you.

Cyberbullying

What would you think if you saw a group of people at school point, laugh, and insult someone who got a new haircut? Obviously, the group of people laughing are being bullies; you know that what they're doing is wrong, it's a no-brainer. But what if you saw a TikTok of someone showing off their new haircut, and when you go to the comments, people are laughing and telling them how bad they look? It's just a video. It doesn't feel real, and you always see comments like that on TikTok. You don't know these people; it's not happening in front of you right this minute, so you can scroll on and never think about it again. It might not be as obvious, but being mean to someone in the comments on a video is also a form of bullying called cyberbullying. The person with the new haircut is a real person with a real life. They see every single mean comment, making them feel just as bad as if the bullies said those things while pointing and laughing at school. When you think about it like that, it doesn't feel so easy to just scroll on and forget about it, does it?

PRO TIP:

Instead of leaving negative comments on the things you don't like, try leaving compliments! You'll brighten someone's day just by saying you like their shirt.

Now, think about how often you've seen those kinds of comments on other videos posted online. Every single one of them is a real-life person being real-life cyberbullied. As a matter of fact, a little more than one out of three people in their preteens and teens have read comments about themselves like that online, and almost one out of every six people in their preteens and teens have made comments like that to someone else online. Maybe it's time to start paying a little more attention to what you say and do on social media, don't you think?

Exposure to Yuck

The internet is truly a place where some people feel comfortable posting almost anything. When it comes to searching for homework answers on Google (that you tried to figure out on your own first, of course), finding recipes, and looking up the release date for the newest pair of Nikes, you're happy that people have put the information online. But some people take advantage of being able to post freely, and you might come across some really upsetting things if you do something as small as accidentally spelling a word wrong or clicking on the wrong website. You might find things not meant for you; people saying and showing pictures of things you REALLY don't want to see, someone physically hurting another person or animal, or other things that are so bad you can't even imagine them. Don't let this scare you away from ever using the internet. Just make sure when you're searching you're careful about what you type in, and especially what you click on.

Online Predators

Cyberbullying isn't the only reason it's important to be careful of what you say and share online. How many people that see what you post online are people that you've met in person? How many of them are strangers that are just your age? Most people really do just want to have fun, share about their lives, and see what others are doing, saying, and thinking. But sadly, some people use the internet for reasons that aren't so good. Honestly, it's easy to lie from behind a computer. It's easy for strangers to use fake pictures and fake names and tell fake stories to trick people online into doing things they wouldn't ever do. These people are known as online predators, and they can be really scary. Online predators are adults using the internet or social media to talk to young kids, tweens, and teens by pretending to be someone else or saying they want something they don't actually want. These people may act like they're your age to flirt with you and send you gross, rated-R pictures. Some online predators will even tell you that they're an adult, so you'll trust them and do what they say, even if you know you probably shouldn't. Don't worry, though; you can definitely still go online and have fun on social media without worrying much about online predators as long as you follow internet safety rules.

Internet Safety

Are you pretty much ready to throw out your computer and delete all of your social media at this point? Don't take it that far. Yes, the internet can be a dangerous place, but only if you don't know how to protect yourself. So let's calm your nerves and talk about the best ways to stay safe and responsible online.

Rule #1: Make your profile private. Don't just turn on the privacy settings on Instagram and let that be it. Really take the whole privacy thing seriously. Never post personal details like your address (the most important one), phone number, school, clubs, or anything about your money. You're private, mysterious, and basically a secret agent. You don't want anyone destroying your mission.

Rule #2: Be careful of requests. Now that you're all private, no matter how cute and sweet their profile picture looks, don't accept any friend requests from anyone unless you've met them in person. Nobody is tricking you!

Rule #3: Think before you post pictures. Take a magnifying glass and look over every inch of your picture before... just kidding, but be sure to look over your picture to make sure there aren't any personal details or anything inappropriate in them. What they say about pictures posted on the internet staying forever is true. Can you imagine one of your teachers seeing a picture of you and your friend throwing up a middle finger? Yikes. If you choose to take a picture like that, save it for only yourself. By the way, no judgment if you do actually use a magnifying glass; better safe than sorry, right?

Rule #4: Block! It's easy to get distracted and accept someone you think you've met in person but find out later is a total stranger. Just block them! Some people call blocking "petty," but I'm here to tell you that those people are wrong. The block button can be your best friend, even if you have met everyone you've accepted to see your profile. If they make you feel weird or unsafe, or just say something negative or mean, BLOCK! You don't need that energy in your life.

Rule #5: Be mindful of what you write to others. Never, ever forget that everything you say online will be seen by other people. Even if something you write doesn't seem mean or harmful to you, someone else may see it differently. While sometimes people really do take things the wrong way, just like in person, make sure you really think about the things you say before you say them...or... write before you write them.

Rule #6: Think carefully about sharing links to other sites. Just like rule #5, just because you don't think a certain site has anything inappropriate or offensive doesn't mean it doesn't. If you choose to post any links, make sure you go through the whole website to make sure you're sharing what you think you're sharing. How awful would it be if you thought you were linking to a website about picking strawberries, but when you scroll to the bottom of the page, you see in big letters, "THIS WEBSITE SUPPORTS DOG FIGHTING"?

Activity

Pick Your Perfect Password

Staying safe online could never be complete without knowing the importance of the password. Creating a good password can be tricky. You want to make it something that no one could ever guess but is pretty easy for you to remember. For starters, even if you have the best memory in the world, write your password down on paper and keep it somewhere safe, aka, right here in this book. There's nothing more annoying than trying to log in to a website, not being able to figure out your password, and having to go through the whole process of resetting your password over and over and over again.

> **PRO TIP:** Never use your name, phone number, or birthday for a password. While they're easy to remember, they're also easy for others to guess.

Coming up with a good password can be tricky. Answer these questions to help get your brain's creative password juices flowing:

MORE THAN STRANGER DANGER: LEARNING THE ROPES OF PERSONAL SAFETY

1. What's your favorite holiday? _____

2. What's the name of your favorite pet? _____

3. In what city were you born? _____

4. Where in the world do you most want to travel?
   _____

5. What's your mom's or dad's middle name? _____

5. What's your favorite word/sentence?
   _____

6. Choose the two best answers you wrote above. Combine the two and make them one long word. (No spaces or capital letters)

Ex: favorite pet + favorite holiday = buddychristmas

Write yours here: _____

Perfect! The first half of your password is complete. Now for part two:

1. What's your favorite number? _____

2. What's your favorite athlete's jersey number? _____

3. What are the last two digits of your best friend's phone number? _____

4. What age are you most looking forward to turning? ____

Choose one answer from the numbers above and write it here:

_____

That number is the second half of your password!

Finally, take the first half of your password and combine it with the second part of your password. Remember, no spaces.

Ex: buddychristmas25

Write yours here: _____

Congrats! You've now picked your perfect password. Don't share it with ANYONE! Well, except your parents, if they ask.

Dealing with Bullies (Online and in Person)

Anywhere that a bully thinks they'll be safe and suffer the least consequences for being mean to someone is where they'll do their bullying, and many times, that place is online. A super important thing to remember about any bully, but especially a cyberbully, is that when they comment something mean on someone's posts, they don't even believe what they're saying. They're only saying mean things because they think it will cause a reaction from either the person they're bullying or someone else. The cyberbully doesn't care if it's a good reaction or a bad reaction as long as they're getting some type of attention. So, if you're ever being cyberbullied, what do you do to make sure they don't get that attention? You ignore them. I know, ignoring someone who's trying to make you mad, hurt, or embarrassed is so hard. All you want to want to do is defend yourself, or maybe even try to get them back, but you know that A) you're way more mature than them, and B) responding with anything other than silence is EXACTLY what they want you to do. Show them that you don't care what they have to say, report them to the social media platform, and give them the good ole block. Most of the time, this will be enough to get them to stop their bullying and leave you alone. However, there are some cyberbullies that just won't quit! If they're absolutely determined to get a response from you, they might bring the bullying from TikTok to Snapchat, Instagram, Facebook, or any platforms they can still get to you. This is when it's time to take action, and no, you still aren't going to respond to them. Instead, you're going to take pictures of everything they're saying and show them to an adult you trust. Don't worry; they'll take care of any steps that need to happen from there.

So, what about when it's not you that's being cyberbullied but someone else? Well, what would you want someone to do if they saw that you were being cyberbullied? You'd probably hope they would stand up for you, make sure you're okay, and show you that they're on your side, right? Then that's exactly what you do for them. It's okay if you don't want to get in the middle of it. You can always help them in private by messaging them. Just ask them if they're okay, remind them that ignoring the bully is the best thing to do, and make sure they know that none of the things the bully is saying are true. Maybe you'll even make a new friend! Sometimes you might feel a little shy or uncomfortable saying anything to the person being bullied, especially if you don't know them very well. Don't feel bad; you can still help them by not liking or sharing anything the bully is saying on your own profile and showing an adult.

In-Person Bullying

Online bullies can really hurt your feelings and tear down your self-esteem, but at least you don't have to worry about them physically hurting you. I mean, what would they do, put their fist through the screen? No chance! It's also a lot easier to silently walk away from a bully online because you have time to calm your emotions before taking the next step. Even if your defenses and anger take over for a few seconds, you still have the chance to backspace any messages you *almost* send. In-person bullies, on the other hand, are right where you are. Not only do you have to worry about them possibly getting violent, but you also don't have a lot of time to calm down, so it's more likely you'll react. Just like cyberbullies, in-person bullies want to get your attention, upset you, and make you fall to their level of immaturity. The worst thing you can do is to give them what they want by saying hurtful words back or getting physical. It's super hard to be able to hear someone say something mean right to your face and be strong enough to turn around and walk away. Controlling your emotions takes a ton of maturity and practice, but I know you can do it. However, if you aren't able to fully control your emotions quite yet, there are a couple ways to respond to them that might help.

#1) Tell them to stop. Bullies HATE it when you stand up for yourself. This is way easier said than done, especially if they make you feel scared, but try to remember your own worth. You are an amazing, strong, independent, and confident person, and you don't deserve to be treated the way they're treating you. Let the bully know that you won't stoop to their level, you know what they're saying isn't true, and they're wasting their time trying to hurt you.

#2) Make a joke. Reacting with humor will really catch a bully off guard. They're expecting you to get angry, embarrassed, or sad, but boy will they be surprised when you start laughing instead! Turn their insult into a joke by laughing along with them. This shows the bully that you're confident enough to laugh at yourself and you don't take them seriously at all.

Even if it doesn't seem like it, bullies are actually very insecure. They bully to try and bring people down so they can feel better about themselves. By acting in a way they don't expect, they'll realize that bullying you only makes them feel worse. It almost makes you feel bad for them, doesn't it? Can you imagine feeling so unhappy with yourself that hurting other people makes you feel better? Don't let feeling bad for them take over and try to be their friend, though. Just try not to be mean to them back, tell an adult about them if they don't leave you alone, and move on with people who are nice to you – those are the ones whose opinions matter anyway.

So, what if the people who are usually nice to you, the people you consider friends, start randomly being mean to you one day? Are they a bully now too? No, probably not. It's important to be able to tell the difference between a bully and a friend that's upset with you or just having a bad day. Remember, your friends are humans, and humans aren't perfect. Like I said before, controlling your emotions is super hard, and it's not uncommon to mess up sometimes when you're practicing learning how to control them. This is a time when ignoring someone being mean to you probably isn't the best thing to do. Ask your friend to talk in private, and see if they'll tell you why they're suddenly being mean. Usually, you two will be able to talk it out and go back to normal. However, it's not impossible for them to keep being mean, and that's where things can get hard. Maybe they refuse to tell you why they're upset, or they say there's no reason at all. Sadly, this is when it's time to stop being their friend, treat them like a normal bully, and tell an adult if you need to. While having someone go from a friend to a bully is hard, think of it as your green light to try new things and find new friends!

Body Safety

"Keep your hands to yourself." How often did adults say this to you when you were younger? Probably a lot, or at least enough to still remember how important it is to not touch other people or things without their permission to this day. Every single person in the world has the right to say when someone can and can't touch something that belongs to them, especially when that thing is their own body. Unfortunately, sometimes people don't respect that right and won't ask your permission, or ignore you when you tell them no. This is called a bad touch. This type of touch is the opposite of a good touch, which makes you feel happy and loved, like your mom kissing you on the cheek when you leave for a sleepover. Bad touches will never make you feel the same as good touches. Instead, they make you feel uncomfortable or even scared, and it's so (X10000) important to know that it's never okay when someone does it to you. It doesn't matter who that person is, whether it be your friend, a stranger, an adult, or even the king of the world, if they touch you in a way that you don't like, immediately tell them that what they're doing is not okay and they don't have your permission to touch you, and then tell an adult you trust. If the person that gives you a bad touch specifically tells you not to tell anyone, then it's *even more* important to tell on them, because that means they know what they're doing is wrong. Don't ever keep secrets with someone who makes you feel uncomfortable, no matter what they say. I know that respecting and obeying adults is normally a big rule, but this is one of those special times when you can break it and not get in any trouble at all. If they don't respect you when you say no to their bad touch, then you don't need to respect and obey them by keeping their secret NO. MATTER. WHAT. After you tell an adult what's happened, do your best to stay away from the person who gave you a bad touch. If you're in a place where you can't leave, like school, then ask the adult you told to help you read your school's policy about bad touching. This is called the 'sexual harassment policy,' and it will tell you everything you need to know about what to do next, like filing a report and keeping a record to make sure the person who gave you a bad touch is punished.

Bad Touch Warning Signs

Answer the five warning sign questions below with a yes or no. If you answer any of the questions with a yes, or if you're not sure about any of the questions, talk to a trusted adult.

1. Do you ever feel like you're being forced into a hug, kiss, or cuddle?

2. Do you feel uncomfortable just being near someone?

3. If you said yes to #1 or #2, does the person making you uncomfortable buy you gifts to get your attention?

4. Do you ever feel like someone is trying to get too close to you?

5. Does someone way older than you hang out with you more than they hang out with people their own age?

Motivation Moment

Remember how we talked about people on the internet forgetting that the mean things they're commenting on are being read by a real person? This is even more true when it comes to celebrities. If you don't believe me, go on Instagram and read the comments on any of your favorite celebrity's pictures. Bullies get *super* jealous of celebrities because they seem to have everything they want – lots of attention. And what's the only way a bully can feel better about someone getting more attention than them? You guessed it, try to make them feel bad. No matter who you are, how many fans you have, or the number of cool things you get to do, someone saying mean things to you will always have an effect, even just a tiny one. Millie Bobby Brown, the actress from Stranger Things and Enola Holmes, was only a few years older than you when she started getting bullied by thousands of people, both in-person and online. Can you imagine? One bully is bad enough, but thousands of them saying mean things all the time? While the comments she hears from her bullies sting at first, she always tries to remember that they're only trying to get her attention and they don't really mean what they're saying. Millie is so used to dealing with bullies she handles them in a way we haven't talked about yet. She doesn't ignore them, ask them to stop, or make a joke. Instead, Millie does her best to spread love back to those who send her hate because she knows that's what they truly need most. Now THAT'S what I call a master at managing emotions.

Chapter 5

EMO DUMPS: MANAGING EMOTIONS EFFECTIVELY

Did you know that your brain can talk to you? No, not with actual words, but with emotions. Joy, sadness, fear, anger, and disgust are all messages from your brain that tell you what you like and don't like, aka exactly the things that make you, you. In the movie 'Inside Out,' 11-year-old Riley learns just how important it is to listen to every emotion your brain sends you. If even just one emotion is ignored, all the other emotions won't be able to send you the right messages, and you could end up forgetting your favorite memories or lose interest in the things you love. Can you imagine not remembering how good it feels to play your favorite sport? Without remembering how much you love it, you might just choose to never play again! So what do you say to making sure that NEVER happens and brushing up on your feeling skills ASAP?

Activity

Getting to Know Your Feelings

When you feel an emotion, do you usually pay attention to exactly what it is? It's easy to forget to be aware of your emotions while you feel them, so let's do that now!

Wherever you are while reading this book right now, close your eyes for a few seconds (unless you're walking. If you're walking, I'll give you the 'keep your eyes open pass'), take a deep breath, and ask yourself, "What emotion am I feeling right now"?

Did any emotions speak up? Did you feel any differences in your brain or your body? If yes, is it one or more than one? Ex: happy and relieved, frustrated and nervous, sad and excited, or maybe all of them at the same time! There's no right or wrong answer(s). Just write down what came to mind:

_____

When you pay attention and become aware of your emotions, they become pretty easy to split into two categories based on how they make you feel. Happiness, curiosity, thankfulness, love, interest, comfort, and excitement make you feel good, so they're usually put in the 'good emotions' category. Sadness, anger, loneliness, jealousy, fear, self-criticism, and rejection make you feel bad, so they're usually put in the 'bad emotions' category. Ugh, I know. Two categories that are so different from each other, how could you possibly choose only one? Don't even worry about it. You get to have them both! Yippie, right? What? You don't want the bad feelings? I bet most people would agree with you on that one. Many people think they can get away from the "bad" emotions by ignoring them, but that doesn't work for very long.

Think of it like this: if you fell and broke your leg, would you just put a band-aid over it and try to walk like normal? No! Maybe the band-aid would make it *look* like you're healing on the outside of your leg, but on the inside, your bone is just getting worse with each step you take. So you have to give your broken bone the attention it needs and help it heal by getting a cast. Ignoring and refusing to feel bad emotions is the same way. You can't just use happy feelings to cover up your bad feelings and expect them to heal. Nobody can, and you know what? That's okay. While you can't cover them up or snap your fingers and make bad emotions disappear, I can tell you a secret: "bad" emotions aren't all that bad. Yes, they do make you feel bad – sometimes really bad... But how bad is something if it can help you learn important lessons? Learning to feel the bad feelings without acting on them is a big part of maturing and growing up. The faster you let yourself feel your bad emotions, the quicker they heal, and you can get back to feeling the good emotions again.

Self-Control / Self-Regulation

Emotions can be extremely powerful. Sometimes they come without warning and can be super hard to control. It takes a lot of practice to be able to keep yourself calm when someone makes you sad, angry, or embarrassed but letting those feelings take over and acting on your emotions pretty much never turns out in your favor. But... almost everyone has at least one moment when their brain goes fuzzy and fire-y red, causing a... not so calm reaction before learning how to regulate their emotions, so don't feel bad if that has happened to you. In fact, you can use it to your advantage by having a specific memory to think back on when practicing self-regulating your emotions with the 5R's:

#1 (R)eframe: You may not be able to slow down time to stop to think like they can in movies, but you can use your memory to try and remember exactly what happened in the moments leading up to your emotions taking over. Were you already feeling stressed because of other things that day? Were there certain words that someone said that caused a switch to flip? Did you feel the need to say something because there were other people around? Most times, there are hidden reasons for the emotional takeover that you may notice when thinking back on the memory. It's important to reframe any thoughts that you may have that tell you you're a bad person for letting your emotions get the best of you and recognize the real reasons, like stress, fear, anxiety, or embarrassment. For example, instead of thinking, "I'm bad for acting that way" you can reframe the thought to "I acted out of embarrassment."

#2 (R)ecognize: Feeling stressed is a common reason for losing your cool, but which stress affects you the most? Believe it or not, stress isn't as clear as you may think. It can actually be experienced in five different types.

- Physical stress: muscles feeling sore after a new exercise, getting a headache from loud music, or getting sick.
- Emotional stress: losing someone you love, moving to a new school, or mental health struggles (depression or anxiety).

- Cognitive stress: worrying about homework or an upcoming event like sports, performances, or tests.

- Social stress: comparing yourself to others, worrying about what others think of you, or not getting along with a friend.

- Pro-social stress: worrying about other people's stress that you have no control over, like your friend not making a good grade on their test, your mom being late to work, or a stranger having a broken leg.

#3 (R)educe - manage your stress: There are so many things that can cause you to feel stress. You can control some of them, but many of them you can't. However, when they're out of your control, there are things you can do to reduce the negative feelings they can cause. Exercises like running and walking can really help you release stress while also being great for keeping your body healthy. If working out isn't your cup of tea, practicing mindfulness techniques can really help take your brain from focusing on stressful things by bringing your thoughts back to the present moment. This can be done by writing your thoughts out on paper and breathing exercises like the 5-5-5 breathing method, which is one of my favorites. You can do this method no matter where you are without anyone even noticing. All you have to do is breathe in for five seconds, breathe out for five seconds, and wait for five seconds before repeating the process. Try to keep repeating the breaths for one minute, then see if you feel better. I highly recommend practicing breathing exercises when you aren't stressed, too, so your body will recognize what you're doing and help you calm down even faster.

#4 (R)eflect – When you start your journey of managing your emotions, it may be a little hard to decide which feelings you're having as a whole. Recognizing your feelings takes a lot of practice because a lot of feelings feel very similar. It's also possible that the feelings you think you're feeling are just covering up what you're actually feeling (whew, lots of feelings). For example, feeling sad or embarrassed can hide behind feeling anger. Since your goal is to get to the bottom of why you're feeling a certain way, it's important to actually know what emotion it is that you're feeling, which is why making an appointment with a mental health professional is always a great idea. They can help you slow down and set goals that are specific to you, so over time, you'll know exactly how to name, manage, and release your emotions in the best way for you.

#5 (R)espond – Practice all your R's! Remember to be patient with yourself. Slow down, take your time, and give yourself space to mess up sometimes. Self-regulating your emotions can be hard work, but I promise the peace and happiness it brings you will be worth it.

If you're up for a challenge, there's one more way that can be super helpful with controlling your emotions, but you have to promise not to toss it out before giving it a try! This one might feel a little bit silly at first, but if you keep doing it, you'll feel way better... positive self-talk. Yes, self-talk as in talking to yourself! You don't have to say it out loud; you can practice self-talk in your head too. You know how it feels great when someone is cheering you on, or taking your side when something goes wrong? Well, this is basically the same thing, or at least that's what the part of your brain that controls your feelings thinks. When you start feeling anything bad, or even just kind of weird, tell yourself what you would want someone else to tell you. Telling yourself things like, "I am strong" and "I can do this" really does work. Try it out!

Activity

Free Your Feelings

Talking about your feelings with others can be scary sometimes, especially when you aren't sure how you're feeling yourself. Other times, you may not feel comfortable sharing something you're going through, but you still want to find a way to manage your emotions. No matter the reason, or the emotion, journaling is an amazing way to walk through your feelings so you can really feel them and let them go.

Your journal can be anything you want. A pile of papers, a book, the notes app on your cell phone, or a recording of you talking out loud. As long as you get your feelings out there, you'll start feeling better.

When you first start journaling, you might find that your emotions take control and fill your page up before you can even blink. You might also find yourself a little stuck on deciding what you even want to write about. Here are some ideas:

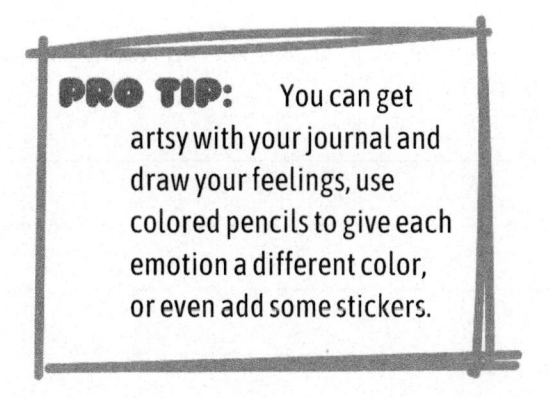

> **PRO TIP:** You can get artsy with your journal and draw your feelings, use colored pencils to give each emotion a different color, or even add some stickers.

1. What's something on my mind a lot recently?

_____

_____

_____

_____

_____

2. When was a time I felt happier than ever?

_____

_____

_____

_____

_____

3. Has there ever been a situation you wish you had handled differently than you did?

_____

_____

_____

_____

_____

Journaling doesn't have to be long paragraphs, and it's not only meant for when you're feeling down, stressed, or angry. You can also journal when good things happen so you can read what you wrote the next time you aren't feeling your best. Your journal is one hundred percent yours, so use it however you want, whenever you want! The more you practice, the easier it will get, and the more you'll learn about your emotions.

Resilience

Have you ever had an adult tell you that your life can't be hard because you're still young? It doesn't feel great, does it? Sure, you don't have bills or a job to worry about, but that doesn't mean every day you live is automatically easy. Sometimes, adults forget what it was like being your age. Growing up has some tough hurdles to get over, and someone telling you that what you think is hard isn't actually hard definitely doesn't make it any easier. You have a lot of new responsibilities and changes happening to you and around you, and juggling everything all at once can be stressful. If some days you feel like things are *too* much, or you don't do as good of a job on something as you'd hoped, remember to cut yourself some slack. You can't get everything right every single time. Getting upset with yourself will only add more stress and make things even harder. Remember that you're not alone! I know it's crazy to imagine, but your parents were once kids too. They've been through a lot of what you're going through now, and obviously, they made it out alive, or else you wouldn't be here reading this! I'd be willing to bet they learned a few things from their own experience that could help make things easier for you. All you have to do is ask. Here are a few things they might tell you:

Create a safe space to relax. Your bedroom is a great place to make your safe space, especially now that it's clean (since you read chapter three). You need a place to go where you can completely forget about tasks and stressors and just turn your brain off sometimes. Your bedroom is already a place where you feel comfortable, and you don't have to worry about anyone interrupting you. Alone time to let yourself just relax is so important in making sure you don't get overwhelmed and let your emotions take control.

Create a routine. Since you're going through so many new experiences, you might start to feel like you don't have any control over the things happening around you. Things that you don't expect are always popping up, and sometimes you just aren't sure how to handle them. It's important to take some control back and create a routine that always stays the same. That way, you'll know of at least one thing that will happen one hundred percent every day, no matter how unexpected the rest of your day is. Your routine doesn't have to be long and take up a lot of time unless you want it to. A routine can be something as simple as stretching before getting in bed every night or waking up at the same time every morning.

Take care of yourself. No matter how crazy life gets, always make it a priority to take care of yourself physically, mentally, and spiritually. Think of your body as a car. Cars need gas to be able to drive anywhere. If you don't fill the gas tank when it's running low, you risk running out of gas completely in the middle of the road, and then you can't go anywhere at all. Your body is the same way. To be able to do the things you need to do, you have to make sure your energy tank doesn't get too empty. If your energy tank is empty, it doesn't matter how many things you need to do; you won't be able to do them.

> **PRO TIP:** Doing things like showering regularly, eating nutritious foods, releasing your emotions, doing things you enjoy, and getting enough sleep are all super important for keeping your energy tank full.

Put things into perspective. Even if it feels like the thing causing you stress will never end, I can promise you, it will. Whenever you start feeling this way, you can put things into perspective by thinking about the last time you felt like a stressful situation would never end. It did, didn't it? You got through it last time, so you have what it takes to do it again.

Help somebody. Nothing gets your mind off your own problems like helping someone else with their problems. Ask your parents if they can help you find places to volunteer, pick up more chores around the house, or help someone learn something new.

Activity

Turn the Block Into a Stepping Stone

Your resilience will really shine through when something unexpected happens, but it doesn't stop you from continuing toward your goal. Instead, you find ways to see the unexpected change of plans as something positive. Can you think of a situation when something happened out of nowhere that caused you to change your plans but in the end, turned out even better than you originally thought? Let's practice some of those situations:

You and your friend have plans to go to the neighborhood pool. It's the first day it hasn't been raining all week, so you're super ready to swim. When you get there, the gate to the pool is closed with a sign that says, "Closed." This changes the plans for your whole day! How will you have fun now?!

Circle the way you can show resilience in this situation.

A) Decide the day is ruined and spend the day being upset inside.

B) Hop the fence and swim anyway.

C) Accept that the pool is closed and get excited to brainstorm another way to have fun today.

Let's go through the choices. If you choose A, you're letting your emotions take control and wasting a beautiful day. If you choose B, you could get in a lot of trouble, or worse, someone could get hurt. If you choose C, you still get to spend the day having fun with your friend, and you might come up with a plan that's even better than swimming.

Now try to come up with your own way to show resilience when something doesn't go to plan! Here's your situation:

It's the beginning of the school year, and everyone is finding out their teacher for the new year. All your friends run up to you with huge smiles. They all have the same teacher! But when you look at your schedule, you find out you have a different teacher than all your friends. Even though you might feel sad at first, how might having a different teacher end up being a good thing?

Write your answer here:

_____

_____

_____

_____

_____

_____

Motivation Moment

Sometimes life throws curve balls that make things ten times harder than you ever expected, and your emotions will really challenge you. Scientist Marie Curie knows a thing or two about those moments as a Polish woman who pushed through discrimination, loss of love and family, and living through a terrible war. No matter the hardships Marie was put through, she never let them stop her, and she went on to be the first woman to earn a Nobel prize! Her experience only shows that even though there are times when managing and overcoming your emotions will be incredibly hard, having the resilience to get through them can lead to opportunities that you never thought were possible. If learning about emotions and pushing through hard times can do something as amazing as help you win a Nobel prize, can you imagine adding time management skills to the mix?

Chapter 6

GLOW UP: STRIVING FOR SELF-IMPROVEMENT

Twenty-four hours in a day sounds like a lot of time, doesn't it? That's enough time to watch 48 episodes of your favorite 30-minute show! Well, as long as you don't need to eat, go to the bathroom, shower, go to school, do any homework, talk to anyone, or sleep – which is impossible. When you think of it like that, maybe 24 hours isn't all that long after all. You take eight hours to sleep, there's seven hours of school, one hour of homework, one hour to eat, 30 minutes to use the bathroom (on average), 30 minutes to shower, and that leaves you with... only six hours left in the day. That doesn't even include things like getting dressed, cleaning, cooking, walking, driving, etc., and it especially doesn't include resting, watching TV, hanging out with friends, practicing any sports, or doing anything you actually *want* to do. Poof! Twenty-four hours gone in the blink of an eye. So, how do you fit in the fun stuff? How do you know when you can do stuff you want to do instead of need to do? That's exactly what the 34th president of the United States, Dwight D. Eisenhower, wanted to know too, and he found the answer: organizing and prioritizing with what he called the "Eisenhower box." This box is split up into four sections to help you organize your tasks by showing you what needs to be done now and what can be pushed off until later. These boxes are: Urgent/Important = something you really need to do by a specific time, Not Urgent/Important = something you need to do but can be done later in the day between the urgent/important tasks, Urgent/Not important = something you need to do, but can be done by others if needed, and Not important/Not urgent = something you don't need to do right now or ever.

Don't worry if you're a little confused; we'll make one together soon so you can really get the hang of it.

Time Management and Organization

Imagine this: One of your teachers gives you homework on a Friday (Ugh. I know.) On Friday night, you don't even think about the homework. Why would you? You still have Saturday and Sunday! Instead, you go to the movies with your friends. Saturday comes, and it's a beautiful, warm, sunny day, so everyone is going to the pool. How could you pass that up just to stay in and do homework? You'll just do it that night, no big deal. You stay at the pool all day, and you're EXHAUSTED when you get home. No way you can pay attention to your homework tonight; you can do it tomorrow. You have all day! But... it turns out that Sunday is chores day, AND you forgot that it's your grandma's birthday, and she's celebrating with a big barbecue with the whole family. I guess you can do the homework tonight when you get home. Not ideal, but that's okay. Except... when you get home, you realize that you have *double* the amount of homework you thought, and you're stuck

GLOW UP: STRIVING FOR SELF-IMPROVEMENT

between going to bed super late and being sleepy all Monday or getting a bad homework grade. If only you hadn't procrastinated and pushed the most important thing off to the last minute... but at least you know for next time. So, what's your first step to making sure it doesn't happen again?

> **PRO TIP:** Write down all your friends' and families' birthdays on your calendar at the beginning of every year – accidentally forgetting someone's birthday is the worst!

Getting a planner! Everything might've worked out if you had done just one thing: remembered Grandma's birthday – which would've definitely been in your planner. Planners are lifesavers. If you have a bunch of things to do, which you do since you're learning so many new responsibilities, there's no way you can remember every single one without ever making a mistake. You're a human, not a computer. The safest thing to do is always write your responsibilities, due dates, and commitments down in the same place, AKA your planner. They can even double as your to-do list! Planners have space to write for all 365 days of the year, so you can use them every morning and list out all you need to do that day while you eat your breakfast so you can start your day with a plan! Woah, did we just come up with a new morning routine? Easy-peasy! But what if you're a night owl that rolls out of bed with only enough time to get dressed, grab a banana, and race to school before the bell rings? Well, then you'll just add making your next day's to-do list onto your nighttime routine instead! Making a to-do list at night for the next day is my personal favorite way to do it. By adding it to your nighttime routine, you can also get everything ready to go, so you don't have to think much in the morning and just head out the door. Either way, when you see everything you need to do side by side on your daily to-do list, it's easier to pick which tasks need to be prioritized. I like to put stars beside my priorities or write them in a different color if I'm feeling fancy. Priorities are things that are really important and can have consequences if you forget to do them – like getting a zero on your homework if you don't turn it in. It's important to know that priorities can also be things that aren't responsibilities but are important to you, like learning how to dance or roller skate. Planners come in all different colors and designs, and some even come with calendars to write down things like test dates, due dates, vacations, parties, hangouts, and really anything you have planned for the future! This will make sure you don't double up on your plans and have to cancel on a commitment.

To-do lists also really help with the mortal enemy that is procrastination. I know how easy it is to keep scrolling on your phone or play just "one more" video game to put off things that need to be done. Once you write your priorities for the day down on paper, they become way more real. Suddenly, doing the 'fun procrastination thing' becomes a lot less fun and a lot more stressful. With a to-do list, you're way more likely to want to get through your priorities as fast as you can to get to the fun things. Then you can actually enjoy them without any stress since you'll be sure you've completed everything you needed to do already. Managing your time takes a lot of practice, so you're bound to find yourself in a situation where you've just run out of time. Maybe you didn't prioritize correctly, forgot about something you really need to do, or just feel too overwhelmed. No matter the reason, don't forget that you can always ask for help. Everyone has to go through the practice round you're in right now, and as long as it doesn't happen *all* the time, nobody will blame you for making a mistake.

Practice the Eisenhower Box

Activity

We've talked a lot about to-do lists, so let's make one! Go ahead and write down everything you need and want to do today (or tomorrow if you're making this at night). Don't forget to look over your calendar to make sure you don't already have something planned.

For example:
1. Go to school at 8:30 a.m.
2. Cook dinner
3. Do homework
4. Shower
5. Dentist appointment at 12:00 p.m.
6. Practice knitting
7. Scroll on TikTok
8. Make tomorrow's to-do list

Now write yours:
1.
2.
3.
4.
5.
6.
7.
8.

EPIC BOOK OF KID LIFE SKILLS

Great! Now you can use your list to separate them into the four categories in your Eisenhower Box.

Remember:
1: Urgent/Important = something you really need to do by a specific time.
2: Not urgent/Important = something you need to do but can be done later in the day between the tasks in the first category.
3: Urgent/not important = something you need to do, but can be done by others if needed.
4: Not important/not urgent = something you don't need to do right now or ever.

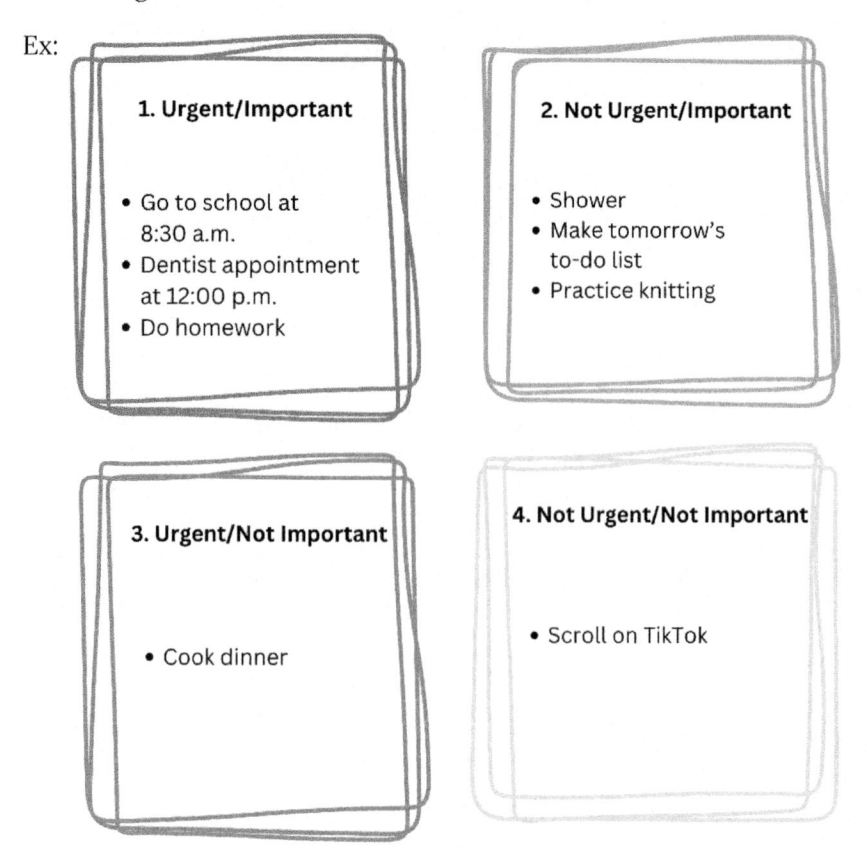

Ex:

1. Urgent/Important
- Go to school at 8:30 a.m.
- Dentist appointment at 12:00 p.m.
- Do homework

2. Not Urgent/Important
- Shower
- Make tomorrow's to-do list
- Practice knitting

3. Urgent/Not Important
- Cook dinner

4. Not Urgent/Not Important
- Scroll on TikTok

Now you try:

1. Urgent/Important	2. Not Urgent/Important
3. Urgent/Not Important	4. Not Urgent/Not Important

Setting Goals

Setting goals for yourself is something you've probably done more times than you can count. Goals to make certain grades on your tests, goals to run the mile in a certain amount of time, goals to raise money for your school's donation rally... but have you ever thought about the work that it takes to achieve them? A lot of times, goals have a long journey. If you don't consider the steps and skills it'll take to get there before setting it, you might not ever reach the finish line. So, how do you fix that? How do you give yourself the best chance at always achieving your goals? Well, you need to learn how to plan your steps to get to your goal, and that might mean splitting your big goal up into little goals and your little goals into tiny goals – whatever works best for you and keeps you motivated. If you're looking to really set your goals up for success, take out a piece of paper – you're taking notes.

(*Announcer voice*) Innnn-tro-ducinggg... the SMART method. You're smart, the method is SMART, so it seems like a perfect match! If you were guessing SMART is an acronym, you guessed right. It stands for the Specific, Measurable, Achievable, Relevant, and Time-Bound Method, but that's pretty long, so we'll just call it SMART. Okay, time to take those notes:

(S)pecific – If you want to achieve your goal, you need to give it some details. What exactly is the goal? What steps will you take to achieve this goal? Do you need help from anyone else to reach this goal? When will you do the steps it takes to achieve this goal? And most importantly, why do you want to achieve this goal? Your 'why' is what will keep you going when the steps seem never-ending.

(M)easurable – While doing the steps to reach your goal, how will you know if they're working? Well, you find a way to measure them by setting up something called a milestone. Your milestones are basically smaller goals that help you achieve your big goal. For example, let's say I have a goal to read 24 books in one year. I can measure this goal by making sure I'm reading a certain number of books each month. Since there are twelve months in a year, my milestone at the end of each month is to have finished reading two new books. If I meet my milestones each month, in January, I'll have finished two books; in February, I'll have finished four books; in March, I'll have finished six books; in April, I'll have finished eight books, etc.

(A)chievable – After you have your milestones, think about if they're *actually* reachable. Do you have enough time in between each one of them? Do you have the free time? Do you have the tools and skills right now, or do you still need to learn new things? If you still have things to get or learn, you can add them into your goal planning as milestones.

(R)elevant – Is this goal helping you to better yourself in the long term? If you have a goal that's going to take a lot of your time and attention to achieve, it's important to make sure it's really worth it.

(T)ime – When do you want to reach your big goal? Put dates on when you want to reach each milestone and your big goal that make sense and work best for you.

There you go! I told you you're SMART.

Look Into Your Future

Do you need a little bit of goal-creating inspiration? Well, do I have the perfect thing for you! You're going to create a vision board. These things are awesome because they combine creativity, motivation, and lots of cutting.

Things you'll need: posterboard, scissors, glue, and magazines.

Step 1: Go through magazines and cut out anything that reminds you of things you enjoy, find interesting, or want to try.

Step 2: Go through all of the cutouts and see if any of them inspire you. Use your creativity here. You may see a purple purse that inspires you to create a goal to paint your room purple.

Step 3: Put the cutouts that inspire you into different categories based on one specific goal. Using the purple room painting goal as an example, you could put cutouts of different colors of purple, a wallet for the money you'll need to save, and a paintbrush.

Step 4: Glue the cutouts onto your poster board, and you're done!

You can put the poster board in a place in your room where you'll be able to see it every day, giving you motivation to achieve your goal.

Developing Critical Thinking Skills

Learning now to develop your normal thinking skills into critical thinking skills is well, critical to say the least. These are the thinking skills that help you make sure you don't live your life simply following the crowd or taking everything anyone tells you as a fact. Don't get me wrong, some of the things you'll hear sound very real, and people can be very convincing that they know what they're talking about, but that won't always mean what they're saying is true. Developing critical thinking skills means listening to what other people are saying, asking questions to learn why they say what they're saying, asking yourself if what they're saying makes sense to you, and then researching it all to read the details of the topics yourself so you can form your own opinions. Learning how to think through things critically is how you'll become a master of solving your own problems, know that you're making decisions that you believe in, and really reach independence.

GLOW UP: STRIVING FOR SELF-IMPROVEMENT

Become a Critical Thinker

Activity

Learning how to develop critical thinking skills doesn't have to be super serious. You can keep it simple with games like tik-tac-toe, word searches, mazes, or my favorite, riddles! Here's some for you to try:

All of the answers will be on the next page, but don't peek!

1. What's something you can catch, but can't throw away?

_____

2. Name four days of the week starting with the letter T.

_____

3. I'm a room you can't enter. What am I?

_____

PRO TIP: If you like exercising your brain with riddles like this, I have good news. There are entire books out there filled with riddles. Go check them out!

Motivation Moment

Have you ever heard of Albert Einstein? You know, that man with the crazy hair that is known to have been an absolute genius? Yeah, that one! He won a Nobel prize for inventing something called the general theory of relativity, which helped scientists understand gravity and a lot of other things about space. Insanely cool, I know, but here's the part that might surprise you: Einstein was definitely a smart person, but he wasn't necessarily any smarter than you or me. Einstein said himself that the reason he achieved his goals is because he took it one step at a time and every day planned and worked toward achieving his goals. It took him a lot of time, and he made plenty of mistakes. But he used those mistakes to motivate him to re-think his steps, and never give up. If knowing that practicing time management, self-regulation, setting goals, critical thinking, and resilience could one day help you do something as amazing as Einstein isn't enough to motivate you, maybe knowing that you also need these skills in emergency situations will do the trick...

Answers to Critical Thinker exercise:
1. A cold
2. Today, tomorrow, Tuesday, and Thursday
3. A mushroom

Chapter 7

IN CASE OF EMERGENCY: HOW TO BE A REAL LIFE SUPERHERO

When you hear people talk about a "superhero," you probably immediately think of someone with powers. Superman, Wonder Woman, Batman, Black Widow, Spiderman, basically any DC or Marvel character. Those characters are cool, and even though it would be awesome if we had someone with powers to protect us from villains in the real world, we don't (that we know of, at least). However, we do still have superheroes among us - I'll bet you even know of a few. Famous actor, Ryan Reynolds, also known as Detective Pikachu, is a perfect example. Do you know what he did to get his official "Superhero" title? He took a class to learn how to do CPR. Choosing to learn how to perform any lifesaving technique is already enough to be called a superhero, but it REALLY paid off a few years later when he used it to save his nephew's life! Ryan didn't think he'd one day need to use CPR to save a life, but can you imagine if assuming he'd never need to use it had stopped him from learning how to do it?

What to Do in an Emergency Situation

When you're in an emergency situation, things tend to happen really quickly, making it super easy to go straight into panic mode. However, the worst thing you can do in an emergency is panic. Don't get me wrong, staying calm in an emergency is NOT easy, but when you panic, your emotions take control, and suddenly your brain is left out of all decision-making. It's extremely important to rely on your brain to use critical thinking during these situations, so how can you make sure you can stay calm enough for your brain to stay in control? Think about it. Have you ever forgotten about a test until the moment your teachers starts passing them out? Do you remember how it made you feel looking over the test and not knowing the answers since you didn't prepare? Now, compare that to a time when you had a test that you studied and prepared for all week before taking it. Which time did you feel more in control when taking the test? Which time did you feel panicked? You can probably see where I'm going with this. If you want to help your brain stay calm and in control during an emergency situation, you have to get prepared.

How to Handle a Fire

Normally when you're in an emergency situation, the best plan is to stay where you are until someone tells you to move. However, this isn't the case when there's a fire. In school, you learn exactly what to do if there's a fire by practicing fire drills. When you hear a fire alarm go off, immediately stop where you're doing, find your closest safe exit, and calmly get out of the building. But have you ever wondered how fires start in the first place? Sometimes, fires are caused by bad electrical wires or natural disasters, but most fires are actually caused by humans – accidentally, of course. Most of the time, when a fire is human-caused, it could've been completely prevented if they had only learned what to *not* do. Let's make sure this won't be the case for you and learn how you can prevent accidentally starting a fire, beginning in the kitchen with the number one house fire cause: cooking. Don't worry; not causing a kitchen fire is pretty easy as long as you simply stay in the kitchen while you're using the stove or oven. Yep, that's all! While a fire could happen while you're cooking, as long as you keep yourself, your attention, and a fire extinguisher somewhere in the kitchen, you can catch it and put it out before it causes any real problems. Want to know what else you can't leave alone without risking starting a fire? Those cute little things that have a wick and burn to rid of bad smells – candles. As innocent as they may seem, they can be dangerous. But as long as you never let them burn any closer than a foot away from something that can catch on fire and never, ever, ever leave them by themselves, you can still use them to get rid of funky smells.

No matter how careful you are, if you're living somewhere on planet earth, there's always a small chance a fire could still happen. Because of this, it's important to have a smoke detector on every floor of your home, especially in bedrooms, as well as a fire escape plan with your family. Be sure to go over that plan every so often so everyone can remember what to do and where to go if there's a fire.

How to Give Basic First Aid

Moving on to your superhero training course – basic first aid. You may already have a first aid kit, but there's still more to learn. In your

EPIC BOOK OF KID LIFE SKILLS

kit, you probably have what you need to treat most nosebleeds, cuts, and burns, but it's important to know *how* to treat them. Of the three, nosebleeds are probably the easiest, so let's start there.

*Please keep in mind that the following information is for minor wounds. Always check with an adult to be sure additional treatment is not needed. *

Nose bleeds: Let's be completely real here. Sometimes you have a booger that's so annoying you just can't stand it anymore! You go in with your toilet paper for the pick and *sigh of relief* much better. But then... you notice that toilet paper is now dotted red, and soon, so is your nose. Don't panic! Rip off a new piece of toilet paper or cloth, pinch tightly right under your nasal bone (a little uncomfortable, I know), and tilt your head back for 15 minutes. If you can, ask someone to set a timer for you so you can know that it's been long enough to let go. Now, remember that there's a cut in your nose, so be gentle and don't blow or touch your nose at all for at least a few hours – try to go the whole day if you can.

Cuts: Speaking of cuts, let's learn how to treat the ones outside of your nose too, because it's a little different. Cuts on the outside of your body leave a tiny opening to the inside of your body, so you need to clean it very gently with hydrogen peroxide to make sure dirt doesn't get inside and cause an infection. After your cut is nice and clean, dab it dry with a clean towel, put on an antibiotic ointment if you have one, and cover it up with a band-aid!

> **PRO TIP:** If you don't have any hydrogen peroxide, gently clean the cut with soap and water. Whatever you do, don't put a band-aid over a dirty wound. It will get infected.

Burns: Since you're cooking all the time now, there might be a burn in your future that will really thank you for learning to quickly put it under cool tap water. Once your burn is under the water, it's going to immediately start feeling way better, but keep the water running over it for at least 10 minutes to keep puffiness down. Now, there's good news and bad news. The good news is that anytime your burn, well, burns, you can use an ice-wrapped towel to cool it down. The bad news is that it's probably going to keep burning at least a little bit for the rest of the day... and possibly the next day too... and you'll probably get a blister. Battle scar! Just kidding, the blister will stick around for a little bit, and then you can put on ointment and cover it with a band-aid to finish its healing.

Alright, now that the first-aid-kit treatable stuff is out of the way, it's time to take things up a notch.

Bumped heads: Some days, we forget we have legs, flop right out of beds, and bang our heads on the floor. All a part of living the life of a human, right? I'm just kidding. Forgetting about your legs probably won't be the reason for bumping your head, and truthfully, any kind of head injury isn't a joke at all. Other than wrapping something frozen in a towel and holding it on the sore spot to keep the swelling down, you're going to want to get plenty of rest! If, after hitting your head, you throw up or still feel dizzy, tell an adult. In that case, it may be time to go to the hospital. But don't worry. That only happens when you hit it really hard.

Twisted ankle: If there's anything that's underrated when it comes to pain, it's a twisted ankle. Sitting down after twisting your ankle is probably your first instinct, but try to ask someone to help you over to a chair if you can. You'll need to find something to prop your leg up so you can lift it up and straight out in front of your chest. Your goal now is to stay seated as much as possible and keep down swelling by wrapping a towel in ice and holding it on your ankle for 15 minutes every hour for the next two days. If it hurts too much, or you can't put any weight on it, take a trip to the doctor to make sure your twisted ankle isn't actually a broken ankle.

Feeling superhero-ish yet? Well, you're about to! Moving on to first aid – level 3.

Choking: Hearing someone coughing for longer than normal and looking over to see that they're choking is nothing less than scary – but you have to take action. Start by asking them if they're okay. If they're able to answer you by making sounds, their airway isn't blocked, and they'll be okay. If they can't answer you by making any sounds, dial 911, put the phone on speaker, and start the Heimlich maneuver:

Step 1: Wrap both arms around their waist, like you're hugging them from behind, and make a fist with one hand.

Step 2: Put the thumb side of your fist right above their belly button.

Step 3: Grab your fist with your other hand while keeping it above their belly button.

Step 4: Drive your fist in and up into their ribcage at the same time in a pumping motion, over and over until the object blocking their airway comes flying out, the ambulance arrives, or you can no longer feel their pulse – if this happens, begin CPR immediately.

> **PRO TIP:**
>
> If you want to get into babysitting, parents LOVE it when you know basic first aid. Be sure to tell them you know what to do in an emergency!

IN CASE OF EMERGENCY: HOW TO BE A REAL LIFE SUPERHERO

How to Perform CPR

While I truly hope you never have to experience a situation where it's needed, learning how to perform CPR can very literally be the difference between life and death. In addition to carefully reading these steps, I highly recommend taking a class to get in-person practice and become CPR certified. Before starting CPR, check for a pulse by taking your pointer finger and middle finger, and putting them on the person's neck right under their jaw beside their windpipe. Press down lightly and wait to feel a pulse for 5-10 seconds. If you don't feel a pulse, begin CPR.

Step 1: Place one hand on top of the chest, and put your other hand on top of the first hand.

Step 2: Using all of your strength, pump your hands up and down on the chest to the beat of the song 'Baby Shark' 30 times. If you're with someone else, ask them to sing the song out loud while you count to 30 pumps, or vice versa.

Step 3: After you've done 30 chest pumps, hold their nose closed with one hand, and slightly tilt their head back so their mouth opens.

Step 4: Breathe two breaths into their mouth, and repeat step one through four until emergency help arrives.

Congratulations, you've completed basic first-aid 101. I may not be able to give you a certification, but you're a superhero in my eyes!

Got Lost? Get Found.

Do you think getting lost is an emergency? I definitely think it could be if you don't know what to do. Depending on what you're doing, what's around you, and how much you're paying attention, you can get lost almost anywhere – I say as I think back to the time I got lost in a parking lot... and a grocery store... and a pumpkin patch... I may have panicked and cried because I had no idea what to do, but that's not going to happen to you, because I'm here to tell you what I now know I should've done – stop where you are, stand tall and strong, and look around. It's possible to overlook your adults if you start to panic, so try to stay calm. Your adults are probably already looking for you, so it's best to stay where you are if it's safe. If you both start looking for each other at the same time, you'll just keep going in circles, and it'll take way longer to find each other.

While you're staying where you are and keeping your eyes peeled, go ahead and call them. If you have a cellphone, use that, and if you don't, literally cup your hands around your mouth, and yell their names. You might attract some extra attention, and someone might offer to let you use their cellphone to call one of your adults' numbers you know by heart. (If you don't know your adults' numbers by heart, this is your sign to do that now.) If you don't get any offers, it never hurts to ask, but be very careful with *who* you ask. If you can, try to look for an adult with kids. This will feel a lot safer, and you can almost be sure they'll be willing to help because they'll know how it would feel if their own kids got lost.

Musical Phone Numbers

I know, I know, your cellphone saves every number you could possibly need in your contacts, so why would you bother memorizing any of them? Well, because things happen, and sometimes those things cause you to be cell phoneless. You could accidentally leave it at home, lose it, it could get stolen, it could break, or the battery could go dead, all of which leave you with zero people to call for help just because you don't know their numbers. Now, don't think I'm saying that you should memorize every single one of your contacts; that would be way too much. You only need to memorize a few important ones, like your family members. Memorizing a bunch of different numbers can be tricky, but what if each of them had their own song? Let's give it a try!

Step 1: Write down three phone numbers you want to memorize. This could be your mom, dad, and sibling, but you can switch it out any way you want.

Phone #1: _____

Phone #2: _____

Phone #3: _____

EPIC BOOK OF KID LIFE SKILLS

Step 2: Write down three songs that you know super well, for example: "Happy Birthday," "Head Shoulders Knees and Toes," and "'I'm a Little Tea Pot."

Song #1: _____Happy Birthday Lucy_____

Song# 2: _____

Song #3: _____

Step 3: Pair all three phone numbers with all three songs and write them together on the lines below. Ex: phone #1 goes with song #1, phone #2 goes with song #2, etc.

1. _____07956 466 274_____

2. _____

3. _____

Step 4: Go to YouTube and play the karaoke version of each song that goes with each number. Instead of singing the words to the song, replace them with the phone number in the same rhythm.

It's easiest to only try and memorize one number with its paired song at a time. Keep replaying song one while singing phone number one until you have it memorized before moving on to the next one. You can practice this for as long as you want over days, weeks, or months. Eventually, every time you sing each song in your head, you'll remember the phone number that goes with it!

Motivation Moment

As we wrap up this supercharged chapter, remember that being a real-life superhero isn't about capes and masks—it's about preparedness, knowledge, and the willingness to lend a helping hand in times of need. From fire safety to basic first aid and even getting found when you're lost, you've added a powerful set of skills to your utility belt. Just like Ryan Reynolds with his CPR knowledge, you're now armed with the ability to make a difference when it matters most. So, take a deep breath, stand tall, and know that you've got the skills to handle emergencies like a true superhero.

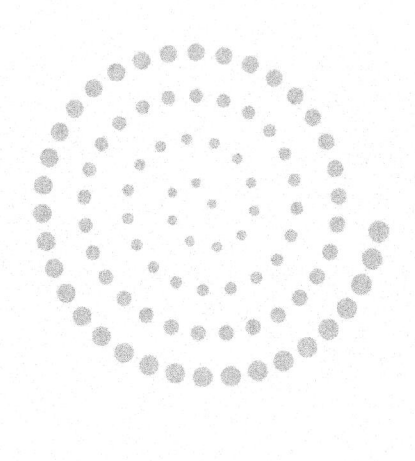

Conclusion

Now that you know how to prevent and prepare for any emergency situation, save lives, and find your adults when... they (totally not you) get lost, do you feel confident that you can let your brain take control when it's best for you? It's safe to say that finding ways to stay calm, showing resilience, and using critical thinking skills will get you through just about every tough situation you find yourself in throughout your life. However, to make sure your brain can take the lead, you have to practice healthy ways to let all of your emotions run free. Emotions are a part of everyday life, for every person in the world, and that won't ever change. Part of maturing is accepting that it's normal to feel angry when dealing with bullies, sad when you decide to spend your money right before finding out that new game you've been looking forward to just came out, or nervous when you get a stain on your shirt – even when you know the steps to get it out. As long as you practice your five R's and learn to self-regulate, eventually, you'll be able to give every emotion the attention it needs without needing to react. Managing your emotions is just like any other new skill you learn; it takes lots of time, patience, and planning. You won't always have time in your schedule to master every new skill on the same day, especially when you choose to do things safely rather than quickly. Besides, spending a few extra seconds to dice your veggies with your fingers in the right position and putting on gloves before taking the dish out of the oven takes a lot less time than taking care of a cut or burn, even when you do know basic first aid. It's important to really do your best to add something you enjoy doing to your schedule every day, even if you have to split it up and only do half of it. However, some days, your to-do list will be full of priorities, and you won't have time to practice the important, but not-so-urgent skills, even if you were to do them quickly.

These are the times that it'll be up to you to find ways to have fun with responsibilities, like turning cleaning into a competition or wearing your bathing suit to wash the car. Other days, you'll have more free time, but you still might need to choose between plans, like dog sitting for extra cash or baking a cake for your mom's birthday – which you wrote down on your calendar to remember (nice job). Speaking of your calendar, don't forget to make sure you budgeted enough in your 'wants' for all the fun things you have planned for this month, while still having enough for 'needs' and 'savings' for your SMART goals. Choosing the right percentages of your money to put into each category of your budget is a huge part in making sure your time-bound goals stay achievable, and your life stays as stress-free as possible.

Well, I think that's it! Not so long ago you were just hoping for some cooking time, and now you've completed the entire learning part of being a responsible, mature, and independent preteen. Now, it's time to put it all to the test! Personally, I think you're ready to tackle all of the opportunities and challenges life could possibly throw at you throughout your preteens, but only you can be the judge of that. If you ever need some motivation, or just a quick reminder of the right steps to take with cooking, chores, money matters, staying safe, managing emotions and time, or any emergency situations, you know where to look. Be sure to share your new skills with your fellow preteens! You can help them become just as independent as you've become by taking a few minutes out of your busy schedule, going online, and leaving a review for this book on Amazon. Don't forget to enjoy these next few years, and try not to think too much about the future because I can't even prepare you for the rollercoaster of your teenage years. Well, actually, I guess I could... Now that I think about it, that's exactly what I'll do.

Good luck, and talk to you soon, preTEEN!

Printed in Great Britain
by Amazon